To]
My ~~Black~~
Varg Vikernes

® & © 2025 Varg Vikernes
All Rights Reserved
Website: www.thuleanperspective.com
Contact: ancestralcult.shop@gmail.com

Dépôt légal, mai 2025
ISBN: 978-2-9596629-4-2

Foreword to "My Black Metal Story"

This book is written solely by me, based on what I remember about the Norwegian Black Metal scene from 1991 to 1993. Sometimes I also fall a bit outside this scope, but by and large this is what the book is about.

I first wrote all I could think about this, and then read through it all to see what was missing. The missing things were added where it made sense, so I jumped a bit back and forth in topic.

The book is not written chronologically, and I also asked people on X (my account: @BornLik23266) to tell me what they wanted me to explain or elaborate on, so in some chapters I will repeat parts of what I have said earlier, because I talk about the same, but from a different perspective and in a different context, and to shed light on something else related to the same.

Sometimes I explain my own views about something, but other times I explain how I saw it back then. This is often hard to differentiate between.

There were until now no book dealing with this topic in a fair manner. They are all written by people with an agenda, often a sinister motive even, and by people who simply put had no reason to believe that they knew enough about this to write anything at all, to begin with.

When I write this book, I will not try to sugarcoat anything or try to present myself or my role in the Black Metal scene in a particularly good light. I don´t care what people think of me, as long as they have the opportunity to make up their opinion based on the *facts*, rather than lies, slander, myths and exaggerated nonsense. I am perfectly okay with not always having been what I would have wanted me to be. Making mistakes is a part of the learning process in life. A part of growing up. A part of your education.

So this might sound a bit strange, but I would like many people who currently *like* "Varg Vikernes" to *stop* liking me, because often they like *the lie*, and not the real me. If I am to be appreciated, I would like the real me to be appreciated. If not, if they do not appreciate me for what I really am, then I would prefer them not to appreciate me at all...

As you can tell already, this will be a personal book. Not only was I part of this scene, even an instrumental part, for better or worse, but my own public personality is very much interconnected with this whole topic. Not only do I know – *know* – the facts about this, but I have the distance and disdain for the whole subject to write truthfully and accurately about it. To destroy the lies, myths, slander, nonsense, and twisting of facts.

Indeed, you are reading my spell of destruction...

This is the true story about the Black Metal scene in Norway, and also my story.

Varg Vikernes
January 2024

Foreword to the 2nd Edition

The language has been improved in some places since the first edition. The oral tone has been preserved, however, to provide a more honest and genuine reading experience. This book comes not only from memory, but from the heart as well! Enjoy!

Varg Vikernes
April 2025

1

How did I become involved with the Death Metal scene?

Ah, so you already wonder why I did not write "how did I become involved with the Black Metal scene"? Yes, because there was no Black Metal scene when I became involved with the *Death* Metal scene in Norway, in 1989.

When I was 14 years old my older brother purchased an electric guitar, and for some reason I too purchased a guitar, from the same seller. I do not know for sure why I did that. I certainly had no ambitions to become a musician, but in any case I did. The reason why is lost even to me. I guess, the only reason I can give would be that the seller had a second guitar that he wanted to sell as well, and it was not too expensive, so...

At the time I went to Karate training a few times every week, I went to the shooting range every week and I had friends that I played roleplaying games with. We kept doing that until I was around 17, and they decided to give priority to their formal education instead (stupid bastards....). Other than that, though, I most of the time played the guitars, in my room. When the others stopped playing role-playing games, I played the guitars a lot more. I had nothing better to do.

The following might sound odd, and certainly would have not worked in a film, because it is just something that does not happen in real life. It would sound too unlikely, but...

You see, one of the girls I went to elementary school with, had a big brother who played in a metal band. One day I had lost my plectrum (pick), and I really wanted to play the guitars, and I came to think about that guy in a band, who lived a few stone throws away from where I lived. So I simply did the most autistic thing, and walked over to his place, called the door bell and asked him, **Harald,** if I could borrow one of his plectrums. I was 17 at the time. I think he was 21. He was in a band, **Amputation**, with **Jørn-Inge**. By chance, his girlfriend was there as well as two guys from **Old Funeral**, and instead of lending me a plectrum, they invited me in – and I am pretty sure (as far as I can remember) that I learned for the first time in my life about what Death Metal was. Until then, I had only ever heard a single song by **Death** on a radio show when at in friend´s car (but I did not know it was

"Death Metal"). Other than that I had only heard of Thrash Metal bands, and listened to **Bathory**, **Kreator** and **Slayer**. I was really impressed with the **Old Funeral** demo tape, as well as the **Amputation** demo tape. By chance they needed a second guitar player for **Old Funeral**, and invited me to come visit them in their rehearsal place the day after, and see if I could start playing with them. And I did.

I can add that they had the odd name **Old Funeral**, because there was another band in Bergen called **Funeral**, and to stress that they were the *first* **Funeral** band, older than the other **Funeral** band, they were the... *Old* **Funeral**. Yeah, their original name was **Funeral**. With time it became simply **Old Funeral**.

2

We played Death Metal until 1991. We also naturally listened to other Death Metal bands, and with time came to the realization that all the bands actively tried to sound the same. Once one band (**Morbid Angel**) had become popular, and had been signed to (as we saw it) some big and fancy record company, all the other bands wanted to sound just like them. Several even went so far as to travel long distances, in order to record their albums in the same sound studio as that one band had used, to get the exact same sound. They all sounded the same. They all looked the same. They all had the same PC lyrics or the same childish "gore lyrics".

What is the point of having all those bands, if they all sound the same? What happened to originality? Integrity? Creativity? Do we really need 6 million different examples of the exact same? Isn´t 1 enough?

In reality, we were kind of ignorant and stupid, because of course that is what always happens when someone is successful! Like **Morbid Angel** was. Their music was really cool, and others wanted to become equally successful, and therefore tried to make the same type of cool music.

If you have a recipe for success right in front of you, most of you will grab it and use it! Simple.

When we one day in early 1991 decided to visit a guy **Harald** corresponded with, **Euronymous**, living in Ski (in Eastern Norway), outside of Oslo, we found that others too had noticed this pattern. And were not happy with it.

His own band, **Mayhem**, had been playing since 1984, and was a complete failure. They did not even rehearse! As he, **Euronymous**, put it: "Our bassist (**Necrobutcher**) is just smoking pot with his girlfriend, and our drummer (**Hellhammer**) is just running around in Oslo screwing sluts." Their vocalist (**Dead**) had locked himself in a room in the house they rented, and had basically stopped speaking to him. He almost only ever left the room to eat.

Whilst other bands were signed and became "famous", his own band did not even rehears! And what kind of bands were signed to big companies!? Bands with bland-looking kids in colorful jogging pants. Their own mini-album, **Deathcrush**, that they had released themselves, was not only sold out, but frankly an embarrassing heap of garbage; some sort of noisy fun-core metal music, but they had since then replaced the drummer and the vocalist, and fairly recently released two tracks on a compilation album, and one of them was really good too (**Freezing Moon**). But that was already old news. Nothing happened with them in 1991. **Mayhem** was in practice dead. Then he saw that those other "poser" Death Metal bands, who had all started long after their veteran band started up, in 1984, had great success at the same time...

Come on! This is called petty envy! But we, **Harald** and me, and the other guys in Bergen (Western Norway), failed to see this, because we too disliked the current "Death Metal trend". For a completely different reason, sure, but still. We all agreed that Death Metal had become a boring trend.

The next day some of the guys from **DarkThrone** came over, with their new record (**A Soulside Journey**), released on a big British record company. They, still in their teens, wore white jogging pants and bland clothing, and **Euronymous** let them hear it. That was *not* how metal bands were supposed to look!

Upon return, as agreed upon when there, I sent some ammo to **Euronymous**, for his shotgun, and after that, he sent a letter to **Harald** telling him **Dead** had committed suicide. After that we did not hear from him in a long time. I think in almost 6 months!

We kept growing increasingly disappointed with Death Metal as a whole, both the guys in **Old Funeral** and the guys in **Amputation**, and in September 1991 I decided to leave **Old Funeral** and instead do something different. I had already made some tracks that were not suitable for **Old Funeral**, e. g. the **Burzum** track (called **Dunkelheit** on the **Filosofem** album), and I figured I could do everything myself. At the same time, **Olve** (from **Old Funeral**) and **Harald** (from **Amputation**) decided to leave their bands and form a new band, **Immortal**. **Old Funeral** continued without **Olve** and me, for some time, I think well into 1992, still playing Death Metal.

Instead of listening only to Death Metal bands, in that period we started going back to listening to older music. Bands we used to like before we became fascinated with Death Metal. Thrash Metal bands like **Destruction**, **Kreator** and **Bathory**. Some (others than me) also started listening to even older styles, that they had listened to before, Heavy Metal bands like **Accept** and even **Kiss**. Also, I listened more and more to underground "white label" house and techno music, and later on (1992) even alternative music like **When**, and I think you can tell from listening to my early records.

In any case: we found inspiration in other styles of music. That is: styles other than Death Metal. This certainly made an impact on our own music.

Sadly, I do not remember exactly when, but at one point **Euronymous** wrote that he had moved to Oslo and had opened up a metal shop there. Some time in November (I think), there was a **Morbid Angel** concert in Oslo, and we decided to use the opportunity to visit his shop, called **Helvete** ("Hell") by the way. Guys from different bands, and with different fanzines from all over Norway showed up, and we learned that **Euronymous** "had had enough" now, and that "those stupid Death Metal kids in jogging pants" were to blame for **Dead**'s suicide. If you wanted to play extreme metal in Norway from then on, you better look metal too! "Death to Death Metal!"

Now, this was of course pure nonsense. **Dead** did not kill himself because other bands had members wearing jobbing pants...

Euronymous also boasted of having taken parts of **Dead´s** skull and made necklaces of them, that he had given to close friends. He further explained that he had taken pictures of the corpse, but had not yet had the films evoked by a photographer. He was afraid that if he went to a Norwegian photographer, it would cause problems for him. In the end, much later I think, he sent the films to the Netherlands and had them evoked by a Dutch photographer, and when he did, he naturally showed these to "everybody" in the scene.

And for the records: no, I never received any such necklace, nor wanted one, and in fact never saw one either. He had given them away long before we had ever visited him in his shop in Oslo.

Because of the success of many "Swedish" Death Metal bands (and because of **Euronymous´** reaction to that), this lead to a rivalry between Norwegian Black Metal and especially "Swedish" Death Metal. These Swedish bands became the embodiment of trendy, multi-cultural, spineless mass-produced Death Metal music, with images of posers with worried faces ("aLL tHosE pOor STarvIng aFriCaNs") in jogging pants on the covers and with politically correct lyrics ("tHinK aBoUt gLoBal waRmiNg, BruH!").

Now this was all fine and good for us in Bergen, because his envious hatred for Death Metal bands and their vast success, coincided with our disdain for the complete lack of originality in Death Metal bands, and not least with our racism (at least some of the Swedish bands had "colored" band members) and disdain for the politically correct image of those bands. So it all kind of blended together, and became a joint disgust for Death Metal, where he picked up our arguments, and we (sadly) picked up his arguments.

DarkThrone had also at the same time just recorded their **A Blaze in the Northern Sky** album, and probably because of **Euronymous´** influence, had just before recording it decided to change the whole (originally a) Death Metal album, into what we today can easily define as *the first* Black Metal album ever. They also looked more "cool", than before (although I think **Fenris** had always looked the same, even when they played Death Metal). Finally some different music! Finally something original!

3

Now, some of you will react to what I just said here: "the first Black Metal album ever".

What about **Bathory** or **Venom**, right?

Well, no, that was Thrash Metal, or I guess in the case of **Venom**, Trash Metal. These bands were never called or understood as "Black Metal" bands. Black Metal as a name for a genre was a term coined by **Euronymous**, inspired by a **Venom** album title by the same name, for a specific group of bands in revolt against Death Metal.

Black Metal was not understood or intended as a music style in itself, like it is today. The thing that made a Black Metal band was the fact that it was completely different in sound *and* appearance from the Death Metal bands. In a sense Black Metal was a term for anti-Death Metal bands. Bands doing the exact *opposite* of those bands that tried to sound like **Morbid Angel** (an awesome band, by the way. Their **Altars of Madness** is fantastic).

The growling vocals of Death Metal was replaced by *something else*. *Anything* else! No, there was no decision on how exactly it was supposed to sound: there was only an agreement on how it was *not* supposed to sound! Not like Death Metal! The sound and production was intentionally made "bad". Why? Because the Death Metal bands tried to make the sound "good".

DarkThrone´s A Blaze in the Northern Sky came in February 1992, and only a month later **Burzum** came out with an album (recorded in January) on **Euronymous´** own record company, and then in September the same year **Immortal** released their first album.

We were all very excited, and unsurprisingly, the new thing, Black Metal, became popular. (That is: popular amongst a very small group of metal heads in Norway.)

Former (failed, or simply very young) Death Metal bands cast aside their style in favor of what became the new style (because only a few albums had been released after all...), and what had started as an anti-trend became a new trend...

Yeah. The people who agreed that Death Metal had become a trend, just... changed trend. Like **Enslaved** and **Emperor**. And they sounded just like **Burzum** or **Immortal**. Or both.

Again, the perspectives were different: to us this was a failure, because the whole point was for bands to come up with something of their own. Not to copy ("rip off") the style of others. Black Metal was not a style in itself! It was an anti-style! To us these new bands, like **Enslaved** and **Emperor**, were not *true* Black Metal bands. They were just copy-cat bands, shedding their Death Metal skin to suddenly claim to be Black Metal bands. Trying to sound like **Immortal** and/or **Burzum**.

T o **Euronymous**, that old veteran in the (failed) Norwegian Death Metal scene, this was just more of the same: other bands becoming "big" and "important", whilst his own band was doing nothing.

So again we agreed that the development was bad. Something had to be done about it....

Euronymous started to literally threaten people, going as far as to have someone drive him to them, to call their doorbell and tell them to stop calling their bands Black Metal bands, "or else"! "I don´t want these damn cowboy-boots-wearing rock and roll-idiots to be a part of our scene!", he declared. One time he desecrated a cemetery, brought with him a small grave stone and in the middle of the night threw it through the bedroom window of one metal guy he did not approve of in Sarpsborg (Eastern Norway). This was serious business to him.

The underground metal scene in Norway was in turmoil. People loved the new bands, and wanted to emulate their style, but they were not allowed to... by **Euronymous**. He sat there, in Hell, his record shop in Oslo, and spewed out his hatred for all those who were not "true".

And I am not proud to admit that we played along. The others, those accepted as "true" by him, played along. We too started to spew out the same nonsense, partly because we had a genuine interest in keeping this new thing pure and good, and free from trends, rip-offs and copy-cats, but also because we were ensnared by his BS. We failed to see his real motives.

But yes, we eventually did. Not just me, but many. I would claim even most of us. You see, when he finally managed to organize some rehearsals for **Mayhem**, and went to a sound studio to record their first real album, he...

Yeah, what did he do?

...he went to the same studio that **Burzum** and **Immortal** had used, travelled almost 310 miles to get there, and did everything he could to get a *good* sound production. So the whole "dark, primitive and grim sound" was for thee, but the "as good a sound as we can possibly get" was for me. That is: for **Mayhem**.

This was in September 1992, I think. He wanted *his* band to become mainstream and popular after all.

He had clearly been playing us all along, and we saw it. We understood. His shining star on the Black Metal sky started fading, and sank steadily into the dark and cold sea of Lies, Hypocrisy and Falsehood...

By the time they were to mix their album, in mid 1993, nobody in Bergen even wanted to let him and **Hellhammer** stay over at their place, for a few days. Nobody had any problems with **Hellhammer**, I think every single individual in the scene liked him, he was a very nice guy, but **Euronymous** was so unpopular at that time, that they did not want anything at all to do with him.

A lot happened before it came to that, though, and we shall talk more about that first...

4

Burzum was signed to his label, **Deathlike Silence**, some time in late 1991. I sent him a demo tape and he liked it, and told me he wanted to release a **Burzum** LP, but did not have the funds for it. So I agreed to borrow money from someone else, to pay for the recordings and printing, and release it on his label.

By that time I had met him twice, and only spoken to him no more than a few minutes or so on one of those (the first) occasions. I had written two letters to him, and received one answer. So yeah, I did not know him very well.

He came over to Bergen from Oslo when I recorded the album, and for the fun of it, I let him play a solo on one of the tracks. Everything was fine.

Once the album was released, in March 1992, it was printed in a bit less than 1000 copies, less than 500 CDs and less than 500 LPs. Since **Burzum** was on his record company, this was now his new "argument". *That* was how metal music was supposed to sound! Yeah!

Perhaps more than the music itself, his promotion of **Burzum** made it such a trend setter for the Death Metal bands (who later jumped on the Black Metal trend). **Burzum** was truly an anti-Death Metal band, and the image of me on the cover was some sort of undead-looking creature in a cloak. Not one single pair of white jogging pants or other bland clothing anywhere to be seen. This was *true* metal!

And yeah, that is the reason why I list **Burzum** as the main inspiration for the other bands, instead of e. g. **DarkThrone**. I am not claiming **Burzum** was better or anything. It was just that **Euronymous** used **Burzum** to promote this new thing, and not **DarkThrone**. **Immortal** too was more important, because **A Blaze in the Northern Sky** was still made as a Death Metal album, and then changed at the last minute to become more dark and grim, so it was somewhat half-hearted as a Black Metal album. **Immortal** was not. **Burzum** was not. Their albums were the real thing.

Ok, all well and good, but...

Burzum sold out after a short time, and he failed to print new CDs or LPs. The demand was (relatively speaking...) huge, but... nah. He simply did not manage do print more albums. He was out of money.

This situation persisted. Nothing changed. After 6 months, he still had not managed to print more copies.

The problem was that his record shop was an economic black hole. He claimed to support only true metal bands, but almost everything he sold was bland, trendy, poser-metal, of that exact same type that he had professed to hate so much. And yeah, he did not sell a lot of that either, and the rent was immense. So when he sold the **Burzum** albums, he used all the money he got from that on keeping his shop from sinking. He also borrowed money from his parents, to keep it going.

By the time, I had kindled in me the idea that I could actually live from making music, so I became more and more frustrated, and I even went to his shop to try help him out for a few weeks. This might sound bizarre, but sometimes he had orders – he also sold music by phone and mail – but failed to send them because.... he had no car. The orders piled up in his office, but he simply were not able to get his ass up from the chair and get to the mail office to send them. It was too far away. So at one point I drove over there, and tried to help him out a bit. Not because I was kind. Not for his sake. But for the sake of **Burzum**. For my own sake! I wanted him to get his shit together, so that he could afford to print more **Burzum** albums. No, I was not worried about him not paying me my royalties, he never did, or that I owed money myself, for the recording of the album. I just wanted him to be able to print more **Burzum** records, and since the first 1000 copies sold in a few weeks, why would he not do that!? It would have solved even his economic problems. It made no sense. Nothing made sense.

An enormous potential was completely wasted, lost, because of his incompetence.

Further, I had more music to release! I recorded 4 full length albums in 1992 as well as a mini-LP. By the end of 1992, only that one single debut album had been released, in 1000 or so copies.

And helping him out did not help. Nothing did. His entire company, both the shop and the record company, was a lost cause. He was truly incompetent. Or if you prefer that; he was lazy.

I am a man of solutions, though, so I simply started my own record company. **Cymophane Productions**, in late 1992. I would simply release my own records. And do all that work myself. No problem.

Now, this was not taken lightly by him. This was *treason*, according to him. He had zero understanding for my own situation, and simply saw it as treason. I was now no longer a band on his label that he wanted to promote. I was *competition*.

At the time, we still talked (on the phone) and tried to sort things out, and he kept complaining that he did not get enough customers to his shop. So when some guys asked me for an interview for a "big" newspaper about Black Metal, I told him about it, and he became very enthusiastic. We agreed that I should try to promote Black Metal and his shop, and to put on a show and make it sound as extreme as possible (to scare away "posers", as he put it....). This would not only help his shop, and thus his label, but also me, because **Burzum** was still on his label, after all. I had not yet released anything with **Cymophane Productions**. So, silly me, I did it... that fateful Interview in January 1993.

The journalist arrived, and agreed to not reveal anything about my identity. I was to promote Black Metal in general and his shop in particular after all. He would interview an anonymous source.

What I did not know, though, was that the journalist was a fanatic Christian, and a particularly dishonest one too. Not only did he massively twist my words, but he also called the police right before he was to publish the interview, to have me arrested, to deny me the opportunity to talk up against anything he wrote.

E. g. He asked me: "What do you think is the most evil thing a man can do?" Naturally, I had not prepared for that kind of questions, and had zero experience with journalists, so even though it was completely irrelevant, I answered and said: "I guess it must be to kill your own parents." When he printed the "interview" it said that "He wants to kill his own parents". That was the level of his journalism. The entire "interview" was like that: a heap of twisted words and with a completely different focus than what had been intended. And I was in custody at the time, unable to talk up against anything.

When the policemen asked me about it, I confirmed that I had indeed given an interview to a journalist, and this was presented in the mass media as: "He *confirms the contents* of the interview" (that I had not even read...).

The level of dishonesty was extreme! I had never seen anything like it. I had entered a scene more putrid, rotten and disgusting than any metal scene I had ever seen: I had entered the scene of modern mass media.

In the meanwhile, because of the attention my "interview" had created, **Euronymous´** shop was overrun with customers!

Sounds good does it not?

Yeah, well.

He closed the shop.

His parents felt that the attention was very uncomfortable, and told him to close his shop, and he did. I guess he had to, because they were the ones giving him money to keep it going.

Not only that, but he put on a white sweatshirt and went to the MSM and *apologized* on behalf of the entire Black Metal scene for all the discomfort we had caused.

I knew nothing about this, when I went to court, wearing a t-shirt with the same image that he had on his shop´s front door, to promote his shop.

The problem was of course that nobody, not one single individual, in the Black Metal scene wanted to apologize for anything at all. Also, I had done that to promote his shop! So WTF was he doing!? The former Black metal hero had become an absolute.... clown.

So perhaps now you better understand why, by the time they were to mix their **Mayhem** album, in mid 1993, nobody in Bergen even wanted to let him and **Hellhammer** stay over at their place, for a few days.

Naturally, I was angry at him too. Not only was he a lying coward, but I had actually made some serious sacrifice for him, by helping him out in the shop, but of course mainly with that interview, that left me in prison for 3 weeks and charged with burning down numerous churches. So I spent 3 weeks in prison for what? For nothing!

I can add that the charges against me were never dropped, but they had absolute zero evidence that I had done anything, so of course it led to nothing.

But in reality what I had done was not for nothing. Black Metal became massively promoted because of this, and

Euronymous was approached by professional distributers, who could not only give his label a better distribution, but also finance the printing of albums for him. Also, he assured us that he had given that interview and had apologized just to get his parents off his back, and that he was in reality "true as f***".

Yeah, well. At least most of us semi-accepted that, and I think the offer from the distribution company was what made me overlook this, and keep working with him. *Finally*, after a whole year, would he be able to print more copies of the **Burzum** album and also finally release the other albums too! I even gave up on my **Cymophane Productions** plans, and handed him all the money for pre-orders I had received for the (mini-) album that he now would release on his label instead, with those new distributors. Silly me.

He took all the money, paid his bills, and never sent any of those who had pre-ordered anything at all. And technically, that was my fault. I was to blame for that. I had trusted him with those money. What a moron.

*The Aske ("Ash" or "Ashes") mini-album, with cover art work "giving the finger to society." Photo by **Are**.*

5

The problem in this new situation was that the mainstream media was interested in talking to me, and not to him. He was no longer the center of attention, as he had been for so long in that scene. He became more and more envious, and I was completely oblivious to that fact. I did not think about it. I think it topped when I was invited by **Earache**, a (to us) big English (mostly Death metal...) record company, to discuss whether they would sign **Burzum**. They talked to me, but could not cope with the fact that I was a "racist" and a "nationalist", and refused to tone that down in any way (they had no problems with me being anti-Christian), so – because of that – they did not want to sign **Burzum**. I was fine with that. I had still been there and talked to them, and this alone made **Euronymous** incredibly envious. His own **Mayhem** had certainly never been approached by anyone, for a record deal.

On one side **Euronymous** would express dislike for me, because he was envious of the attention I got, and on the other side, I would agree with others, when we talked about how weak and coward **Euronymous** had been in this whole case. When he learned about how I "talked shit" about him, for what he had done, and at the same time noticed how more and more people in the scene disrespected him and openly expressed dislike for him, he developed a stronger and stronger hatred for me. He had been the star in this scene, and now, because of *me*, he fell like a rock to the ground. He had become a laughing stock. People did not want anything to do with him. He had become "not true" himself...

...and it was all my fault. As he saw it. Not his actions. Not his weakness. Not his hypocrisy or dishonest. No. It was *my* fault!

In the end, he sat there in his shop, almost entirely alone, with very a few friends left. Like I said, when he was to mix their album in mid 1993, nobody in Bergen even wanted to let him stay over. He had to rent a room in a hotel to be able to do it. He had no friends in Bergen anymore. Not one single.

At the same time, he saw newspapers write page up and page down about me, about **Burzum**, and about other bands too. It was too much for him...

6

He decided that since it was all my fault, I had to "go". If I could be removed, he would get his position and his status back. He talked with his few friends left about how he planned to murder me. He told them he had ordered a stun gun from the USA, and he would use it to knock me out, tie me up and put me in the trunk of a car, drive me out into a deep forest, tie me to a tree and then torture me to death, whilst filming it.

Personally, from March or maybe April, until August 1993, I ignored him completely. Then one day in August he called me on the phone, and with a sugar-sweet voice suggested that I should come visit him, and bring the contracts with his record company (now with new distributors) – that I had not yet signed.

Later *the same day*, he called again, but his childhood friend, **Snorri**, was there, in my apartment, and picked up the phone. The tone was a completely different one. He told him that I had to "go", and **Snorri** waved me over, to let me listen directly to what he had to say. So I heard it from his own mouth, we could say, that he intended to "get rid of me" permanently. He wanted to use the unsigned contracts to lure me over to his place, and then he would "get rid of me." He needed me to sign those contracts first, though, because otherwise he would not be able to cash in on my music. I guess he intended to create another myth around me, like he had done to **Dead**, to promote his own band.

Snorri was living in my apartment, temporarily, until he found some place to live, so the fact that he picked up the phone would not have been that strange, but the fact that **Euronymous** assumed that I was not there or could not hear what he said... is very strange. Maybe he just trusted his childhood friend. I do not know. He certainly had no reason to, though. A lot of things are strange in real life, for sure.

Snorri too was fed up with **Euronymous**, but he was still his friend and even the new guitarist in **Mayhem**. His loyalties were nowhere, though. It is very hard to understand what happened in his head at the time. He was disloyal to *everyone*, even to himself.

After the conversation, I was naturally upset, and wondered what to do. We had already rented three VHS videos from a rental shop nearby, and had pizzas in the oven, and another friend was supposed to come over later that evening.

I decided to sign the contracts and simply hand them over, when he was not expecting it, and thus was not prepared to execute his plan to murder me, to take away any and all excuses he had to contact me or have anything at all to do with me. (Royalties from the **Burzum** albums would come directly from the distribution company, btw.) I was going to leave for his place on my own, all alone, that same evening.

When the third guy showed up, he and Snorri went down to take a smoke. When they came back up, **Snorri** said that he wanted to come with me. He had some new riffs to show **Euronymous**. (He was in his band, after all.) I thought that it was a bit strange, but had no objections. So we both left for Oslo, that evening. The 9th of August, 1993. The third guy stayed behind, to watch the films we had after all already rented and to eat the pizza(s). It took somewhere between 6 and 8 hours of driving to get there, I may add, and we took turns driving.

Now, this is where things get complicated, because according to the police, I left Bergen for Oslo to *murder* **Euronymous**.

According to police interviews, Snorri and the third guy planned, whilst smoking outside my apartment, for the latter to use Snorri´s credit card in Bergen during the night, to give him an alibi.

Honestly, I have no idea if this is true or not, as I was not there, and thus knew nothing about it.

But he "forgot" to give him the credit card, so... that never happened.

Also, without either Snorri or me knowing of it, the third guy claimed (in police interviews) he put on my clothes and "walked around in Bergen", so that people should notice him and think it was me.

This he actually did. However; probably not for that reason. In reality, he had done similar things before, in an attempt to get female attention. Yeah: his idea of hitting on women was to pretend he was me... I am not sure if I should be proud of the fact that I was popular with the other sex, so much that other guys pretended to be me in order to get their attention, or if I should be ashamed of belonging to the same species as individuals who did such things... In any case: I really do not think he did that in an attempt to give me an alibi.

Oh, and I knew about this, because one time in 1993, some girls came up to me and said, about him: "That guy is pretending to be you." They too thought it was really weird. Especially considering that I was actually present. Another time some other girls told me the same, only he had done it when I was not present. "He does it all the time", they told me.

Yeah. What a clown world. And why did I keep him around as a friend after that? Good question.

Back to the "evidence" in the murder case.

Further, they claimed (in police interviews) that **Snorri** came along to call the doorbell and talk in the speaker, when we arrived at the apartment complex where **Euronymous** lived, because they argued that "he would *never* have let me in", considering his plans to murder me and all, if I had showed up in the middle of the night.

But he never did call that doorbell or talk to him through the calling system. I did. And he did let me in. So...

They also claimed (still in police interviews) that I planned to show up, and just walk up to **Euronymous** and cut his throat.

But I never did...

...and the knife I did have on me and that I did use to kill him was *blunt*. It was like a small stiletto (with a 3 inch blade, I would say). Pointy, but completely blunt. It would have been close to impossible to cut his throat with that knife.

It does sound cruel, though, and probably did make an impression on the jury.

But this was it. This was the murder plan. That was never carried out.... and that would not have been possible to carry out either, with the knife I had on me.

Therefore, even if this plan had been real, I really should not have been convicted for premeditated murder, because I never carried out the assumed plan to murder him.

Let me elaborate a bit here about that: according to the law, if you e. g. plan to shoot some guy, and when you show up at his place, he attacks you before you have the time to shoot him, before you even draw your pistol, and then whilst fighting him you draw your pistol and actually shoot him anyway, that is *not* first degree murder, because you did not carry out your plan to murder him. This is just intentional homicide/second degree murder. And if your life was in danger, if he tried to kill you in this situation, you can even claim self-defense!

Like I have said over and over again, and just like **Snorri** told the police in interviews with them: "Something went wrong." This is what I had told him, **Snorri**, after I had killed **Euronymous**, when we left his place, got into the car and drove away.

Now, you can think that something went wrong *with the plan*, but in reality something went wrong *when I showed up*.

I called the doorbell, he replied from the 4th floor (I think), in his apartment complex, in the speaker. He told me "It is a bit late." It was 3 a clock in the morning. I said "I have brought the contracts." He said nothing, but peeped me in.

Snorri stayed behind, to finish his cigarette downstairs, because he was not allowed to smoke in **Euronymous´** apartment. (Because that makes sense, right? You go to a guy with plans to *murder* him, but you respect his policy of no smoking in his apartment?!)

When I had climbed the stairs he stood there, still in his underwear, holding the door open. He pretended that everything was all fine between us. We went into his living room, and I handed him the contracts. He looked at them, to see if they were signed. They were.

Things were not all fine between us, though, and I was probably a lot more aggressive than I should have been. When I told him to basically "f*** off" and stay away from me, pointing my finger at his face, he panicked. He dropped the contracts and kicked me in the chest. I easily pushed him back and in the process threw him to the ground. For a moment both of us considered what to do next, and when he looked at a visible kitchen knife in the kitchen, and suddenly got up and ran for it, I quickly fished up my own blunt stiletto knife from a pocket, moved to block his access to the knife in the kitchen, and stabbed him. Half-heartedly, I have to say, because this was a pretty dramatic (and to me new) move, after all. He then charged for his bedroom instead, where I believed that he had a shotgun and also the stun gun he had ordered form the USA. (If I recall correctly, police investigation showed that he had the shotgun, but not a stun gun. It had not yet arrived from the

USA at that point.) So as I saw it, my life was still in danger. I naturally assumed that even though he was not prepared for it right there and then, he intended to carry out his plan to murder me. So my life was indeed in danger.

Instead of trying to get to his bedroom, he took a right turn and ran out into the hallway. I managed to stab him at least once on the way out, in his upper left shoulder. This time I did not hold back. I had crossed that line. Blood would spray from his shoulder when I pulled the knife out again, and I was surprised by just how bloody it was.

When he opened the door, we saw **Snorri**´s face, lit up by the light from his own lighter. After he had finished his smoke, he had climbed the stairs, but was not really sure about where exactly the apartment was, so he had climbed up one story too much, and ended up in the attic. So he had walked back down, and since the light was out in the hallway, he lit his lighter in an attempt to read the door sign, to see if this was the right apartment.

He was absolutely shocked by what he saw, and looked like a terrified ghost. Still with his lighter lit in front of his face, as we both ran past him.

According to police interviews, **Snorri** completely panicked and had a "black out" at that point, and did not remember anything else until I later on, several flights further down, asked him: "Are you okay?" (No. "Går det bra?")

Euronymous continued to run, but then stopped to make a stand one flight down. Maybe he thought that **Snorri** would help him. Personally, I believed that, because I had no idea where his loyalties were. So I had one enemy in front of me, and one potential enemy behind me. **Euronymous** tried to punch me, but I blocked his punches with the hand that held the knife, so in effect when he swung his fists at me, all it did was to land a stab from my knife to his arm (bicep).

Snorri still stood frozen in front of the front door, probably still with his lighter lit.

Euronymous then made a run for it again, and started screaming "help" and banging the doors that he passed on the way down, as well as the walls. "Help!"

I followed, and kept stabbing him in the one part of his body that I could reach as we ran downwards: his upper shoulders. I was still worried about **Snorri** helping him. Again, the amount of blood spraying the walls when I pulled the knife out after an attack was surprising. It was a lot more bloody than any horror film I had ever seen depicting it.

When he reached the 1st floor he smashed a glass lamp on one of the walls, probably unintentionally, and probably because he was banging the walls, to wake up other residents in the apartment block to get them to help him, and he then slipped and fell into the shards of glass, now all over the floor. He literally landed, in his underwear, in a pile of glass shards.

The autopsy report claimed that the cuts he got from this were inflicted by me, including one under his foot sole. As if I had stabbed him under his foot. Which of course made no sense whatsoever, but their job was to demonize me, so...

You have a cut under your foot sole? Could it come from the glass shards on the floor where you later got up and stood bare-footed, or is it a knife cut from the guy you fight with? Hm.... hard to tell. Right?

"23 sTaB woUnDS, bruh!"

No. But understand that people who fight for their lives are filled to the brim with adrenaline, that will keep them going even after they have received wounds that will later on lead to their death. And yeah, some people can die from a fall from a chair, whilst others can survive being shot 3 times at point blank range with a .375 Magnum revolver. That is just how things are, whether we like it or not.

Anyhow.

I slipped past him, and readied myself for more mêlée. **Euronymous** was trying to get back up on his feet, when **Snorri** came running down the stairs. I immediately understood that he was no threat to me, as he just ran past me, with a completely pale face and panic in his eyes.

This is the moment I "woke him up" from his panic, by saying: "Are you ok?" He was pretty far from being ok.

In the meanwhile **Euronymous** had gotten back up on his feet, and because I was standing in the stairs leading down, I was a little bit under him, and he tried to kick me again. He missed and I countered by taking a step up and thrusting my blunt knife through his forehead. He immediately collapsed, fell down to a sitting position and exhaled – like people often do when they die. His eyes rolled backwards. The knife was still stuck in his forehead, so I jerked it out, and doing do no longer held his dead body up in a sitting position, and he slowly fell forwards as I turned and ran, worried about Snorri, who had the car keys, and who looked like he was in total panic. What if he took the car, and left me there, all covered in blood?

As I ran I heard a large bang behind me, as **Euronymous´** dead body rolled down the stairs and landed on the flight below. If the other residents had not heard anything before, they sure would have heard *that*, I thought to myself, and ran towards the car.

I caught up with **Snorri** by the car, quickly took the keys from him, and told him to drive back to Bergen. Personally, I was covered in blood all over my upper body, so I figured it would not be too smart for me to do the driving. I got into the backseat, and lay down and told him to drive.

After a short while I realized that **Snorri** was lost, in Oslo. He had no idea where to go, and was in fact on the way to Trondheim – his own hometown - and not even remotely near Bergen. I threw the knife out the window on the high way northwards, and told him to take a left turn, in order to find a way back to Bergen.

We found a way leading to Hønefoss, which could lead us on to Bergen later on. Before we got there, we stopped by a lake and I washed most of the blood off me. I tied rocks into the bloodied clothes, and threw them into the lake. That is, i literally swam into the lake, and dropped the bundles on the deep side of the lake. They sank deep into the mud on the lake floor, and most were never found.

When **Snorri** later on showed them the lake, the police used divers but found only one single t-shirt, with the text: "Norway – Land of the Vikings". There was no technical evidence to be collected from it. There was no evidence it was mine, even.

Jørn-Inge had thankfully on one occasion left one of his **Kreator** sweatshirts on the floor in the back of my car, and I was happy to find it there, all dirty and stepped on on the floor in the back, and I put it on. **Pleasure to Kill**, it said, ironically.

From then on, I did the driving, and we figured we should tell the third guy, still in my apartment, that something had gone wrong, and that he should go back home, before the police showed up. Naturally, I had no idea whether or not I had been seen in Oslo or anything, and there was no reason for him to be involved in t his.

We stopped by a phone booth in Hønefoss, but there was a whole gang of teens there, so we continued on, until we found another one. **Snorri** went out of the car and tried to make the call, when a patrol car drove past us. The cop looked at us, as if we had done something wrong. **Snorri** came back, telling me that the phone did not work. In hindsight, I guess the teens we saw at the other phone booth had broken it intentionally, and someone had called the cops. And therefore the cop looked at us that way, standing next to the broken phone booth. The teens had already moved on to the next phone booth. To break that one too.

At this point, of course I intended not to get caught, and expected no justice, so I told **Snorri** to hurry back into the car and drove off. I could see the cop turn around his patrol car behind me, 180 degrees, two hundred or so yards up the road, to drive back to us.

If a cop had stopped us at this point, there would be no doubt that I would get caught for having killed **Euronymous**, so I figured I could just as well try to get away. After the first turn we came to, I stepped on the throttle, and drove like a madman, and...

... lost the cop.

Honestly, I do not even know if he tried to pursue us, because we left in a hurry after the first turn we came to, and never looked back. But lose him we did.

But of course; now they truly must have been on to us, I thought, and maybe he had recorded the license plate or something. Since **Snorri** really had done nothing wrong, I asked him if I should not let him off at a train station in Gol, on the way to Bergen, so that he could safely get on a train instead. I was sure that they would have a roadblock or something further ahead, at one point. There was no reason for him to get into trouble too. I was alone on this, after all. He turned the offer down.

We stopped later on, when we found another phone booth, that actually worked, and **Snorri** told the third guy that: "Something went wrong in Oslo." And I think also: " **Euronymous** is dead."

But nothing happened. I just drove all the way home. No cops. No roadblocks. Nothing.

When I finally came home and hit the rack, after having driven to Oslo, northwards towards Trondheim, then south-westwards to Hønefoss, and finally back west to Bergen again. I was of course dead tired! Shortly after the phone called, waking me up, and some journalist asked me about my opinion on the murder of **Euronymous**. I was of course still exhausted and dead tired, and told him that: "I really don´t want to talk about that now."

The next day the newspapers gloatingly wrote that: "Varg Vikernes is crushed by the news of the death of his friend **Euronymous**".

Yeah...

Then after some hours **Hellhammer** called me, and asked me directly if I had anything to do with the murder of **Euronymous**. He kind of understood already, which of course made sense, considering that **Euronymous** had plans to murder me. So why would I not have defended myself and actually killed him before he could carry out his plan, that I am sure **Hellhammer** too knew perfectly well? I of course had to lie and said no, whereupon he replied, that he could not care less about what had happened. He then literally said: "He he. More money for me" (from the album that was to be released).

Yeah, those who knew **Euronymous** were all pretty fed up with him and his BS.

According to police interviews, the third guy, in my apartment when **Snorri** called him, took steps to make the neighbors believe I was there. He e. g. used my noisy (electric-mechanical) type writer, to write meaningless gibberish, but to make it sound to the neighbors as if I was there, writing. He also played loud music. It is not at all clear whether or not he did this before or after **Snorri** called him, so no, this proves nothing. And playing loud music in the evening and night is not exactly something metal heads *never* do commonly... and for other reasons.

Come to think of it, I think I actually – before I drove home to sleep – first drove to the third guy´s apartment, to see if he was okay (and not arrested) and told him the same, namely that "Something went wrong" in Oslo. Again, I must stress that ending up in a fight where you kill somebody quite correctly can be described as "something went wrong". This is normally not a situation where things are all fine... It does not have to mean that some murder plan went wrong!

The cops found my signed contracts on the floor, in **Euronymous´** apartment, so of course they understood that I was involved. But there was no evidence against me.

They quickly moved their investigation to Bergen, and started interviewing people in the scene. With a focus on **Snorri**, the third guy and me. I told them I had mailed the contracts to **Euronymous**. The date written on them, making this unlikely, because it takes some time for letters to reach their destination after all, were simply wrong. I had no idea what date it was, I (correctly...) argued, and had just written something more or less correctly.

They asked me if I normally wrote the address on the envelop, but I understood where they wanted with this, so I said sometimes, and sometimes not. You can off course see the print from a pen on the letter inside, if you write the address on the envelop with the letter inside. There were of course no such prints on those contracts.

As a curiosity, I can add that we normally greeted each other with "Heil Hitler" and a fascist salute, at that time, and I also did that to the cops, when I was called for an interview. They were a little bit distressed by it.

One time I was called for an interview at an exact hour, but when I came there they were not yet done with the third guy, so when I after having knocked opened the door to their hotel room, he was still there, and the cops later claimed I had "pretty much broken in during an interview, said Heil Hitler, smacked by boots together and given them the fascist salute, and demanded to talk to them."

I guess that is also a way to look at it...

They quickly found out that **Snorri** was the weak link, and they got nothing from either the third guy or me. Unbeknown to me, who could not care less about what had happened, **Snorri** was horribly shaken by the whole event. Ok, I killed some asshole who planned to torture me to death. Should I rather have wanted him to

51

have killed me? I had done nothing wrong. I slept like a child.

Snorri, though, was a wreck. He could not sleep, he could not eat, or do anything at all. So the cops put all the pressure on him. They called him for interviews, again and again, probably followed him if he went outside, and basically broke him even more.

In the end, they picked him up for an interview around eleven in the night, or around midnight, I am not sure exactly, and **Snorri** broke down completely. He wept and cried like a baby, and kept doing that for more than an hour and a half. He was so broken that they were unable to get anything sensible from him. He just cried.

Finally, after an hour and a half or so of crying, he confessed: something had gone wrong in Oslo, he said, and I had killed **Euronymous**.

They arrested two friends of mine along with me, as we left a club in Bergen around 2 a clock in the night. When we arrived at the police station, they let one of my friends go, but kept the other one. That was the guy I call the third guy, in this book. They asked for my name, for the records. In defiance I said "Adolf Hitler". They stripped me naked and threw me in a holding cell. They kept the light on and people kept walking back and forth, policemen and others in custody alike.

I smiled to myself. Is this supposed to break me down? They would get nothing from me.

The problem was that they treated the third guy the same way, and he was completely broken by it, and confessed to everything! Just like Snorri had done.

That is...

They said nothing about any plans to kill him, but admitted that something had gone wrong in Oslo and I had ended up killing **Euronymous**.

They released the third guy the following day. He talked to **Harald**, who later on told, in police interviews, that the third guy had been so relieved to tell the truth to the police, as this secret had been such a burden all that time (one week).

So he told them the truth?

Remember that...

The next day they threw me a track suit, and a pair of socks (but no shoes), and I was walked in irons to a civilian police car parked behind the police station, in the yard. The lead tactical investigators were there, and they asked me: "How do you handle this?" (No.: "Hvordan takler du dette?") I answered: "With silence." And I never spoke to them again.

As we started driving, they started small-talking, to soften me up, but I just ignored them. "Would you like something to drink?" I said nothing. "Are you hungry?" I said nothing. They kept on with similar questions for about an hour, until one of them lost it, and started shouting and screaming at me, and tried to get back to me whilst we were driving. The other two had to physically prevent him from attacking me – he was in the front passenger seat and I was in the seat behind him.

I laughed inside of me. Victory. Those MFs would not get any info from me.

They had of course placed their best tactical investigators in a car with me, for a "friendly" 6-8 hour drive, to get me to talk. But it failed. Miserably. When we arrived in Oslo, they placed me in Oslo Jail, and I never heard from them again. They had given up already.

They did not need me to talk, though. They had **Snorri** and the third guy, who were more than willing to talk and spill the beans. Their problem was that there was zero evidence against me, but plenty of evidence of **Snorri** having been there. Now, this never even crossed my mind at the time, and it took many years to even understand that this was their worry, but they were afraid that I would put the blame on **Snorri**. If I had done that, **Snorri** would have been convicted for this, and I could have walked.

That is, unless they did something about that...

And they did. They went to the third guy, who had already told them what he described to **Harald** as "the truth", and told him that poor **Snorri** would be convicted for this, unless he gave them some more info. "Do you really want to ruin his [**Snorri**] life for something Varg has done?" They did the same to **Snorri**: unless he said something to implement me in this, *he* would be convicted for this crime! Both of them played ball with the cops, and voila!

This is the moment they came up with the idea that I had planned to kill Euronymous before I even left Bergen for Oslo.

The cops also told the MSM that they had my fingerprints in blood from the crime scene. Now, as the one who was there, I know that they did not, and that they just made that up to make sure I would be found guilty, by the people, by the media, before I even arrived in court.

I guess **Snorri** told them that I had not worn gloves, so they felt free to make up that lie.

When in court, I may add, they never brought up this piece of evidence. I guess because it was... fabricated.

In the end, when I went to court, they all were prepared for me to blame **Snorri**, but like I said, the idea had not even crossed my mind. Maybe I was too stupid to come up with such a plan. I would like to think that I simply was not that much of an asshole. What kind of *Untermensch* would do such a thing anyhow?

So when I simply stated in court what had actually happened, like I have done in this book, they were all caught off guard. And note that everything I said, and everything I say here in this book, corresponds completely with all physical evidence in this case. If anyone ever tries to tell you otherwise, they are lying to you.

I told them that he had attacked me and I had ended up killing him. I also told them that I understood that according to the laws and rules of Norway, I had gone beyond my right to self-defense, the moment he started trying to run away instead of continuing to fight me, and that legally speaking I was guilty of what in English is called intentional homicide. That is: you kill somebody, but did not really plan to. However, I had of course done that in self-defense. To save my own life.

I continued to make it perfectly clear that **Snorri** had nothing to do with this case, other than the fact that he by chance was there when it happened. He did not assist me in any way or had anything at all to do with this killing!

The court took a break to the next day. I return to Oslo Jail, and when the other guys heard about what had happened, from radio and TV, they clapped my shoulder and gave me credit for having taken all blame myself, and for having completely talked **Snorri** out of it.

The next day it was **Snorri**'s turn to give testimony, and...

Yeah.

He stuck to the original anti-Varg plan, and claimed we had planned the murder. Naturally, the third guy did the same, and perhaps interestingly, he was never even charged with that. So he participated in the planning of a murder, and also assisted the murder, but he was not even charged? Very strange. He spent a total of one night in custody for that.

And no! This is not how it works in Norway. If you commit a crime, and get caught for it, you cannot "cooperate" with the cops to have them *drop* charges. At best you can get a reduced sentence, but that is it. So yeah, it is really strange that this guy claimed to participate in the planning of a murder, and in assisting afterwards. No.

So they both claimed I had planned to murder him, and they had both assisted me, in driving me there, providing alibi back in Bergen and in helping covering it up.

I will talk more about the trial later on in this book.

In the end here, I will add that the next day, after **Snorri** gave his idiotic testimony, the guys back in Oslo Jail were shocked, and seriously asked me if the guy was retarded, or something.

He basically talked himself out of freedom and into participation to a first degree murder.

What, other than what I have already told you about this, made him do that?!

You see, he had called about 30 (!) medical witnesses who were supposed to testify that he could not do time in prison, for medical purposes. So in his mind, he would walk no matter what. He could say all of this, because he really believed that he would not have to do time in prison anyhow – just like what happened to the third guy, who spent *one day* in custody for this.

One doctor, specialist and you name it, after the other, were called to the stand, and explained us all about all the medical problems of **Snorri**. He was allergic to pretty much everything, including daylight, he was this and that, he suffered from this and that, and frankly, I am not even going to tell you about all of these things, because they are private.

In spite of all this, though, when I ("of course") was found guilty of having murdered **Euronymous**, he too was found guilty of having participated in the planning, and assisted me, and was convicted to 8 years in prison. His entire medical corps had been ignored and he too would have to do hard time.

Knowing that, it makes more sense why the two were willing to give false testimony against me, or if you believe in the police version of all this: why they testified against me even though I had actually cleared them from the case already.

The third guy was not even charged with this, so he had nothing to worry about, and **Snorri** believed whole-heartedly that he was not going to do any time no matter what.

When **Snorri** received his sentence, he was completely broken. He had not expected that at all. 8 years in prison for having done... nothing.

Karma is a bitch, I guess. At least to some.

7

One thing that most people do not know, is that the lead police investigator in this case, the guy who convinced both **Snorri** and the third guy to claim in court that I had planned the murder, and the guy who convinced the church burners to confess and put the blame on me, was also the lead investigator in another well-known criminal case in Norway.

The **Birgitte Tengs** case. A case where a young Norwegian woman was raped and murdered.

Why is this even relevant? It certainly had nothing to do with the Black Metal scene!

You see, this investigator was apparently very good at making people give false testimony. He even managed to convince **Birgitte Tengs'** own cousin to confess to the crime, even though he apparently had nothing to do with it.

Her cousin later on said he had been manipulated by the investigator, and the police found this to be true, and discovered that illegal and immoral methods had been used by the investigator. They also discovered that these methods had been used consequently by him, for years.

Birgitte Tengs was raped and murdered in 1995....

The police then used the investigator as a scape goat, and threw him out of the criminal police, and sent him into service as a normal uniformed patrol cop, in a small town in Western Norway. Everyone were shocked that Norwegian police had used such methods!

Oh dear!

(They all acted really surprised by this.)

The investigator was then personally attacked and harassed, by MSM for a long time, and nobody defended him, especially not the police (who claimed that only *he* had done that, of course, and that they had removed the rotten egg, so everything was fine in the police department now). The MSM persecuted him so intensely and for such a prolonged time that he actually eventually killed himself. Yeah. He committed suicide.

In the meanwhile, I sat there, in prison, wondering if anyone would remember that this guy was also the guy who manipulated the church burners as well as **Snorri** and the third guy into giving false testimony against me.

Nah.

Never happened. They all agreed that in my case: all police interviews had been done correctly.

I am not so sure about that myself, I have to admit.

And mind you: even if we assume that **Snorri** and the third guy *were* telling the truth, that I had indeed planned to murder him, they would still deprive me of actual justice (because I never carried out that plan, so legally speaking it was not a first degree murder) and they even deprived me of the right to have a motive for doing so!

You see, although it was made perfectly clear during the trial that **Euronymous** had plans to torture me to death whilst filming it, and also that I knew about it, not least after **Snorri** had let me listen in when he told him on the phone about his plans to get rid of me (something he testified about in court), they concluded that I had: "An incomprehensible motive". Yeah. Evil Varg had for no good reason whatsoever just murdered that poor and innocent **Euronymous** angel!

I killed, or if you like their version better, murdered, a guy who planned to murder me. In fact, a guy who planned to torture me to death whilst filming it. Damn! I had all the right in the world to kill/murder that piece of shit!

"It is praiseworthy to do what is right, not what is lawful", as the Romans put it.

Also, it is not like I killed a model citizen. I killed a convicted criminal (ha had a conviction for violence, for cutting some guys with a broken liquor bottle in a street fight), a guy who boasted that he had poisoned and murdered a Polish fan, a guy who watched snuff films and hard-core porn, a guy who (at best) desecrated the body of his band member, **Dead**, when he found him dead. I say "at best", because some (probably erroneously) claim he even killed him himself, and made it look like a suicide, or at least (more correctly) drove him to suicide – like the MSM did to the lead investigator in my case. **Euronymous** was a guy who was a *parasite* to everyone around him.

I am still waiting for my diploma from the state of Norway.

You are welcome!

8
Back to January 1993.

The problem, if we can call it that, with my newspaper interview was that Black Metal not only became popular, or the fact that **Euronymous** had completely wimped out, with his white-sweatshirt apology interview, but also the fact that I was in prison during the height of the media storm.

How was that a problem?

Well, the MSM could not talk to me, in my prison cell, and **Euronymous** was obviously worthless as an interview object, so they went to others. Not to actual Black Metal bands, but to the "posers" and "clowns", whom often had even been openly made fun of by **Euronymous**. He needed them as customers, so he smiled and were so kind with them when they came to his shop, but the moment they left, he would trash talk them and make fun of them.

These guys were under **Euronymous´** influence, though, but kind of went too far. They were a bit over-the-top eager to look "metal", so to speak. One of them, a guy **Euronymous** had named **Fisken** ("The

Fish"), because he according to him was so ugly he looked like a fish, came in there with 5 inch nails from his home-made arm guards, and... I happened to be there one time this happened, and I was sitting there talking to **Fenris**. We looked at each other and I am sure we both thought the same, because we started talking about corn flakes, and discussed whether or not they should be crispy, and the metal guy looked like he was about to implode. That was *not* trve kvlt, at all. Here he had "the Count" (my nick, at the time) and **Fenris** himself in front of him, and we discussed... corn flakes.

That type of "Black Metal" heads were interviewed by the MSM, and the Black Metal we know of today, is a result of that. Their ignorant, uninformed version of Black Metal was what became pushed by the MSM. They were picked up from the street, so to speak, and presented to the people: "Look at what Black Metal is all about": 5 inch nails from your arm guards, stupid looking leather boots and walking around in Oslo, wearing corpse paint at all time.

So, naturally, when I came out from custody, I learned that this was not something I would pursue further. I tried to "save" Black Metal for some time, but it was a lost cause. The term was no longer what it was meant to be, but had become a parody of a few poser bands that had actually not even been part of the scene to begin with. Yeah: buying a record in **Euronymous´** shop every now and then, or ordering a record from him by phone, did not make them part of the Black Metal underground scene. Sorry guys.

Eventually, as early as in March 1993, I gave up and instead tried to distance myself from the whole scene, and recorded **Filosofem**, my first anti-Black Metal album...

My idea was that, ok, we had created Black Metal, but by then it was already twisted into the unrecognizable, broken and unfixable, so... move on! Create something else instead. Forget Black Metal. I never cared much for that name anyhow.

Filosofem had absolutely nothing of what the MSM described as "Black Metal", save of course the fact that it was still (mostly) metal music. No "Black Metal" imagery or lyrics. No cringe images of me. No edgy clothing. Nothing. Yet, my fate was sealed, and the album is today considered as one of the most important influences to Black Metal.

I give up.

Let me add an important point here too, though: what I say about **Fisken** above also shows how unfriendly and petty, dishonest and rotten the scene in Oslo around **Euronymous** was. **Fisken** e. g. had done nothing wrong per se, all he did was to enjoy metal music and tried to fit in amongst a bunch of assholes, whom he sadly looked up to and I would argue was misled by, but should have shunned away from instead. He was faced with exaggerated friendliness from **Euronymous** as long as he was there, as a customer, and then mocked mercilessly by **Euronymous**, and the others too, the moment he left the store.

This was not a group of cool guys. It was a bunch of assholes, me included (the times I was there), who (for some time) danced to the pipe of **Euronymous**, an absolute Loser, only because he was older and seen as a veteran in the metal scene. I am glad I lived in Bergen, 310 miles away, and only visited that cesspit a few times.

Also, this type of metal heads were a result of **Euronymous´** own standards, of how a metal head was supposed to look! They were like that because of him, and he mocked them for it! Note that no matter what these guys had looked like, they would have been rejected by **Euronymous**, because his whole point was to find an excuse to reject them. None of them stood any chance! They were all *competition* to him.

9

This is not the first time I try to write about the "murder" case. When I did in the past, in form of blog posts or internet articles, the MSM claimed that I wrote about it to "boast about the murder." I described what happened, in an attempt to dispel myths and lies, but no... according to them I "boasted". They also interviewed the prosecutor from my case who managed to say that what I wrote was "completely new" to him and that I had "changed my story." So of course nobody should pay any attention to it! Their dishonesty was absolute. I have said the exact same all the time. The only thing that has changed is the amount of detail I have included every time I have spoken. Of course, because you cannot include all the details in all situations. One time I could say that I used a "knife", another time I could stress that I used a "short knife". Ok. That is not exactly the same. But no, I never "changed my story". I have never had anything else to say, than what I say here in this book. This is what I say, because this is what happened. This is what I say, because this is what I know.

The truth is that the whole case was extremely politicized, and I was turned into an example by the system. They decided to crush me, me in particular, to set an example, to "scare straight" the others and to have an end to the wave of church burnings that we saw in Norway from 1992 an onwards. When I fight back, they see it as a nuisance, and they use their rotten-to-the-core, corrupt and criminal tools, the MSM and their "legal" system, to keep destroying me.

They have no intentions of admitting any error on their part.

To ensure my total destruction, the whole court proceedings were rigged, from start to finish. They hand picked jury members, judges and even our defense lawyers, and the MSM worked as they intended: as a dishonest tool to support their crime against me. I never stood any chance. When I was acquitted by the jury from one of the charges (the Fantoft stave church case), the main judge was horrified and said that: "He is obviously guilty in that case too, but to spare the public of the costs of another trial, we will not ask for a new jury and a new trial. This will not change the punishment regardless." She had already decided what I was going to get, in terms of sentence – even though she had two co-judges who theoretically should have a say in that to.

The jury was made up of Free Masons, Christian fanatics (including the one and only "Christian Healer" in Norway at the time, who claimed he could "pull the disease from your body by help of Jesus Christ!") and pensioners. Snorri´s lawyer was a drunken Free Mason, who managed to step up in the witness box to testify against his own client, when at one point it was suggested that his client had made up his story after police had manipulated him. He testified, and assured them that his client indeed had participated in planning a murder... so...

Fantastic defense job, Sir!

The court psychiatrists were a self-declared Communist and a "Holocaust survivor", **Karl-Ewert Hornemann**, a Jew who spent three or so years in Auschwitz during the war, and by chance was also a Free Mason – all of them members of the same Masonic lodge. My own defense lawyer was a homosexual who later on argued for pedophilia in public. Myself, I was a publicly known "Nazi".

During the trial, I was denied any opportunity to defend myself. Not by the judges, not by the prosecutor even. Not even by my own defense lawyer! Although if he had allowed me to, I would not have been surprised if the judges or prosecutor had protested and put a stop to it instead. They had no intentions of letting me defend myself!

When witnesses were called to testify, they had all been conditioned for 6 months by the MSM and police, and lied blatantly and poorly, and I pointed out to my defense lawyer that it was extremely easy to prove that. He told me: "Hush! Later. We will do that later." But of course, there never was any "later". They testified, spewed out their lies in court, and I was never allowed to say anything about it – not even via my lawyer, who refused to.

Character murdering me was of course not just accepted, but expected, and the norm for the corps of journalists present as well, who spewed out one infantile character murder after the other, but the moment my own lawyer tried to point out that **Euronymous** was not exactly an angel, **Snorri**´s drunken Free Mason lawyer protested and demanded that: "No ill word shall be spoken about the dead" in court. So the fact that **Euronymous** was a degenerate criminally convicted pervert, who boasted of having poisoned to death a Polish metal head, was never a topic of discussion. According to what was allowed in court, I basically had murdered a kind, caring, innocent and productive Norwegian citizen.

As I have already said, **Snorri** had been turned into a tool of the prosecution, and said everything they wanted him to, even after I testified first and completely lifted him off the hook (he too was charged with murder!). His own father, who was present in court, was so shocked by the coward and dishonest behavior of his son, that he approached me during a break and said that: "That boy (his own son!) has zero backbone." (No. "Den gutten har ingen ryggrad!") He shook his head in despair and sat back down.

So of course I was convicted. Of course I was found guilty on almost all charges, and the one I was acquitted of was even in this atmosphere not possible to pin on me. They had *one guy* who claimed that I had told him that I had burned the Fantoft Chapel. A guy who "by chance" knew perfectly well where *he* had been that night, and who "by chance" had slept in the living room, so that he could sneak out during the night without waking up his brother, who slept in the same bedroom as he did. Other than that all they had were *rumors*, hearsay spread by **Euronymous**, who had used the Fantoft stave church fire to promote **Burzum**, by saying to everyone that I had done it.

Now, his story made sense, in the sense that he explained that he had been supposed to participate in the attack on that chapel, but "the other guy" in on the plan (me, according to him), never came to pick him up and did it on his own.

Nice story, bruh. Not even that kangaroo court believed in you. I was acquitted.

When the judge read up the sentence, she had completely ignored almost everything I had said, twisted everything and basically just made up things. E. g. I had made it perfectly clear in court that no, I was *not* a "Satanist", but she managed to write that I was. Because they had decided that I was, so... who cares about reality, right?

When she came to the conclusion, and eagerly and with visible ill-will told that I had been convicted to 21 years in prison (the maximum possible penalty in Norway at the time), I could but smile. What, did she expect me to be surprised by that? Did anyone really believe I was going to get anything less, after the MSM had been claiming for half a year already that I not only was to be given maximum penalty, but that I obviously also deserved it. Did anyone expect anything less, after that Masonic show in court? Did anyone expect it, after half a year of intense character murder of me by a unison MSM in Norway?

Yeah, not one single journalist did his job. Not one single journalist questioned anything done against me. The only – *only* – article that came in support of me during those months, and even the years after, was an article in a student newspaper in Bergen, where it was written that I had been convicted for "first degree murder" in a case where anyone else would have been convicted for "second degree murder", and that I was given 21 years for a crime that others would have been given 9 tops. That was it. Thank you Norway.

I can add that my own lawyer was at the time declared 100% unfit for work by a doctor, who claimed he had heart problems. The judge decided that this was irrelevant, and could not postpone the trial anyhow, so that I could get a new lawyer. Of course. I mean; they had already decided the outcome before it started, so why bother?

Interestingly enough, my lawyer healed suddenly after the trial, and Norway never again heard anything about his health problems. I do not know what happened there, but I suspect that he had come under pressure from the authorities, and was told to do a bad job, and he really did not want to, so he tried to escape this problematic situation by producing medical papers proving he was unfit for work. It did not work. They forced him to (not...) do his job anyhow. Like I have said all the time, this trial was a scam, the outcome had already been decided before it started, and I would not have felt any less unfairly treated had they just dropped the whole trial and sent me the conviction by mail. That would have been more honest of them, really, instead of pretending that they tried my case in a court of law.

You might think that I appealed and had my case tried again, but... you see... they sent my case directly to (yeah) the "court of appeal". So how would I be able to appeal, when the case had already been tested in.... the court of appeal!?

Nah, my case was tried *once*, in the court of appeal. That was it. I could appeal the length of the prison sentence, that was it. I did, to the high court, but "of course" they argued that I deserved that, at least.

In the MSM they were horrified, though, because I had "only" been given maximum penalty. You see, in Norway they also had a system where you could convict people to "safekeeping" (No. "sikring") - a name for a way to imprison people indefinitely. The MSM had been arguing for this for six months, and instead I was "only" given a prison term.

Disappointing, don´t you think?

With this "safekeeping" system, they could have given me another 10 years, that they would have been able to renew two more times, so in all an extra 30 years in prison.

The problem, though, was that they needed me to have "permanent injury to my spiritual capabilities" in order to do that to me. And since I neither drank alcohol nor took drugs, and since I was not diagnosed with any mental disease, they were unable to do that to me.

Note that this was a strictly legal term, and not even remotely a psychiatric term, but it was used commonly in Norway at the time, and had been before too. The best known example is probably that of **Knut Hamsun**, Norway´s most famous and probably greatest writer in modern times, who after WWII was character murdered by the system, because he had supported the National Socialists, and was said (by them) to have "permanent injury to his spiritual capabilities". Yeah right.

Now, this might sound strange to many, but this is common practice in Communist countries. They *diagnose* their opponents, to discredit them, and use that as an excuse to send them to mental institutions (in effect: prison). Norway did the same, because Norway is the North Korea of Europe. Some sort of illogical combination of a Christian Communist Capitalist Monarchy.

They did something much similar to me too, though. Ok, I did not have "permanent injury to my spiritual capabilities", but because I did not have their Christian values, they managed to define me as having "temporary injury to my spiritual capabilities." That does sound horrible after all. The things that made them say this about me, was that I was a racist (and fine with that) and argued that it was perfectly fine to kill in self-defense, like I had done. I felt no guilt for having killed that poor angel, **Euronymous**. Obviously I did not have a Christian moral.

Of course this has since then been used against me, to *prove* that I am basically a retard. It is a strictly legal term, and has nothing whatsoever to do with psychiatry, but...

The actual psychiatrists in court were surprisingly positive, though, even though one was a Free Mason and a Jew, and the other a Communist. They really had very little "bad" to say about me, other than that my racism seemed genuine, I did not have a Christian moral and that I was somewhat immature. E. g. I was still playing with swords with friends, at the age of 19. (I am 50 now: I still do.... and it is called HEMA: Historical European Martial Arts.)

Other than that, they described me as very knowledgable in a wide range of fields, highly intelligent (also with reference to a clinical IQ test I had taken in junior high that proved this), very polite, patient and willing to listen to other arguments.

When I later on tried to get leaves from prison, and had to (unlike the other prisoners who asked for the same...) go through an examination by a specialist in clinical psychology and a psychiatrist (in Trondheim), to see if I was a psychopath, they confirmed all the positive things said by the court psychiatrists, but also actually argued that the claim that I had had "temporary injury to my spiritual capabilities" (again: actually a strictly legal term) was highly unlikely. This had obviously just been used just to discredit me.

Since we are on the topic, I can add that when I was scrutinized by them, I was not found to be a psychopath. On a scale of 0 to 10 I was a 1, and that 1 was explained by the specialist by the fact that I had been locked up in a cell for about 10 years (by then), and that this naturally would make me a bit egocentric. I mean, who else are you going to relate to, when you sit there in a cell on your own, year after year?

I still struggle with this, I would argue. You could even say that *now* I really *am* "spiritually injured", but by the prison system. And even more than a decade after my release, I have still not healed from all that isolation.

The specialist in clinical psychology was also rather shocked, by the fact that even 10 years after my conviction, the justice system in Norway still described me as a "Satanist". "Varg Vikernes believes in

Satan", they wrote to her. That is what the judge had written in the conviction, after all...

On that cord, let us mention briefly the justice system, and how they claim prisoners need to "build trust" whilst in the prison system. In order to be allowed to get different privileges (better cells, a more open prison, leaves, etc.).

I spent more than 15 years there, and had to give them urine samples almost all that time, sometimes every single week, to prove that I did not take drugs, and not one single of those urine samples were positive (to drugs), and yet they never stopped taking urine tests. They never trusted me not to take drugs. They never stopped treating me like a junkie. So much for "building trust".

When nobody in the Black Metal scene, save at times **Fenris** and also the guys in **Mayhem**, have stood up for me, it is because they are so ashamed of how they behaved in 1993 and 1994, after I had been arrested. They let themselves be massively manipulated by the MSM and also by the police, and they literally ratted each other out, like total cowards, and also confessed to all sorts of crimes that there was no evidence they had done. Instead of admitting this they try to blame me for what happened.

Fenris and **Mayhem** on the other hand, never ratted anybody out, and never behaved like complete cowards in relation to the police, so they feel no need to trash-talk me. They also knew perfectly well that what I did to **Euronymous** was perfectly justified, whether I actually planned to kill him and murdered him or just ended up in a situation where I killed him in self-defense. They know that it was either him or me. And they are glad it was him.

10

You might wonder why **Euronymous** would spread rumors about me having set fire to the Fantoft stave church. Actually, regardless of whether I had or not.

This has to be understood in the light of his wish to keep others away from the genre, the purity spiraling, and the wish to promote the bands that already existed as the only "true" Black Metal bands. I mean, if you have to go to such extremes to be "true", then how many will actually be "true"? Your own band will remain the only "true" band!

I was foolish too, because I never did anything to stop him from spreading such rumors, and I never did anything to argue against what he said. I was perfectly fine with being promoted by him as "true". And yeah, he did because **Burzum** was on his label. I mean, if the "truest" band was on his label, that meant he could promote himself and his own label as the "truest" as well. This would confirm his own status as the one individual being able, or if you will allowed, to declare other bands as "true" or "not true".

The truth is, I never said anything to him about having burnt down Fantoft stave church. He just *assumed* that I had done it. Also, when others asked me about it, I neither confirmed nor denied it. One of the many metal heads interviewed by the police told them that he "knew" that I had done it! "How?", the police asked him. "Did he say so?" The metal head responded confidently that: "I know because he did *not* tell me." Somewhat confused, the police asked him: "What do you mean?" He replied: "I knew because of the way he smiled when I asked him about it."

Yeah, that is going to hold in court....

There were *hundreds* of interviews by the police, of different moronic metal heads in Norway, claiming they *knew* I had done it, because "**Euronymous** told me he did it". All of them manipulated by the MSM into hating me and wanting revenge for my murder of their *hero*, **Euronymous**!

The police must have been rather exhausted, by all these morons, and in the end only a handful of witnesses were called to testify in court. The rest had nothing but hearsay and rumors and mind-numbingly stupid nonsense, to say, like the example above shows. (I know, because I had the dubious pleasure of reading through all the police interviews in this case, before the trial.)

In the end, I was convicted for having set fire to four different churches. But I was acquitted in the case of Fantoft stave church. There was literally zero evidence suggesting I had done it.

The problem is of course that there was really zero real evidence in the other cases too. They certainly had no physical evidence. But what they had, was the guys who had admitted to actually setting fire to those churches. So, as the police suggested to them, why not implement *me* in those crimes too, to get a sentence reduction for themselves?

Bard from **Emperor** admitted to having set fire to Holmenkollen chapel. So all he needed to do was to say that "Varg participated", and I ended up with a conviction for it too. **Thomas** of **Emperor** admitted to having set fire to Skjold church. So all he needed to do was to say that "Varg participated", and I ended up with a conviction for it too. **Jørn-Inge** from **Hades** admitted to having set fire to Åsane church. So all he needed to do was to say that "Varg participated", and I ended up with a conviction for it too. **Padden** from

Old Funeral and **Jørn-Inge** from **Hades** admitted to having set fire to some church tower (also in) Fantoft. So all they needed to do was to say that "Varg participated", and I ended up with a conviction for it too.

Easy.

That was it. That was the evidence. That was the *sole* evidence they had against me. This is the sole reason why I was convicted for these "crimes!"

The reason I was not found guilt for having set fire to Fantoft stave church too, was the fact that they never found anyone who admitted having set fire to it, so they had no witnesses who could implement me in the crime.

When another lawyer, many years later, reviewed the evidence, in relation to another trial against me, in 1997, where I was to be convicted to also pay compensation for damages I had caused (because being convicted twice, and be punished twice, for the same crime is perfectly in accordance with international law, right?), he said to me: "How on Earth did they manage to find you guilty in these cases? I mean, you *obviously* did not do it." He pointed at the fact that **Jørn-Inge** and **Padden**, who both played in the same band at the time, had even scouted out Åsane church, to see if they could break into it (to steal some music equipment there), one week before it was burned down. **Jørn-Inge** then argued that I had picked him up one day, from the street, when he was outside a rock and roll pub in Bergen, along with **Padden**, and then I had driven towards Åsane and told him: "We are going to burn down Åsane church". Naturally, he was too weak to say no, because I had such a strong personality. When nearby I turned off the lights on the car we drove, a VW from 1987, and drove closer to the church.

My lawyer argued that: "You cannot turn off the lights on a (Norwegian) car from 1987. Legislations came in Norway some years before that, where it was made mandatory for all cars to have the headlights connected to the ignition. So when you turn on the ignition, the lights come on. To turn them off, you need to turn off the ignition. **Padden,** on the other hand, whom he was out with, in Bergen, drove a Ford from 1980. A car that did not have the lights connected to the ignition. Hm...

Also, **Padden** had been filmed by the police, when he was watching the church burn (seemingly laughing himself half-way to death, and struggling to make a cigarette, because he was so excited).

How would he know, my lawyer argued, that this church in Åsane, was going to burn, if I had only told the other guy about it in the car, on my way to Åsane?

Further, **Padden** then drove to my place, to tell me the news, that Åsane church was burning.

Why would he do that, my lawyer argued, i f **Padden** had been told by me before hand, that I was going to burn the church? I would have already known, would I not?

Also, there was never made any good argument for why I should have wanted to bring **Jørn-Inge** with me, if I was to burn that church. He was drunk. He said himself that he did nothing when there. I had driven the car. I had turned the lights off. I had carried the gasoline to the church. I had broken in. I had poured gasoline out inside. I had broken in. I had set fire to the place. I had done everything. Even the judge was a bit perplexed by this: "So what were *you* doing, whilst Vikernes was doing all this?", she asked him. "I was running around, screaming Satan and stuff", he said.

Yeah, that sounds very useful. And smart. Carry on **Jørn-Inge**...

Padden was of course never even charged with this, and instead **Jørn-Inge** and I were convicted.

Now, I have no problem with **Padden** not being even charged with this. There was no evidence suggesting he did anything here. He obviously knew it was going to happen, and really enjoyed it a lot, but it ends there. Anyone other than him could have driven a **Jørn-Inge** to the church in a car from before before 1985 or so, and the fact that he drove out there to watch it burn even suggests that he did not do it himself. I don´t think he would have done that, if he had set fire to it himself.

However, why on Earth was *I* found guilty in this case?

Jørn-Inge was found guilty because *he confessed*. Had he simply said: "Nah. I dindu noffin", he would have walked away, with no charges even. The same applies to all the others who were convicted in Norway for having set fire to a church. They all confessed. There was zero physical evidence in any of the cases. They simply confessed. They doomed themselves, with their own weakness and stupidity.

Why did they confess?

Because they were duped by the police. The police simply said things like: "We know you did it, we have evidence. You can confess now and we will go easy on you."

"Okay, I admit it."

Case solved.

Although, let us not forget that they were interviewed by that policeman, who were scapegoated by the police and MSM for having used illegal methods to make people confess too...

The police also promised them leniency in the legal system if they could pin these crimes on me. Any crimes, actually. **Bard** from **Emperor** even testified in court, under oath, in 1997, saying: "The police told me they wanted to get Varg and asked us to produce all the evidence we could against him. They even told us to blame him, to get away with shorter sentences ourselves."

Of course the judges completely ignored that, and the fact that now suddenly nobody testified against me (they changed their stories, refused to testify or simply did not show up in court at all). Instead of using testimonies given in court, the judge used my old conviction and police interviews (!), as evidence to have me convicted (for the same crimes, again) anyhow, to pay for the churches that had been burned down. I was convicted to pay the equivalent of 5 million USD with a 12% interest.

My (sarcastic?) mother offered them the rights for my ultra-racist, anti-Christian a n d revisionist **Vargsmål** book, so that they could publish it and make money from it, but – unsurprisingly – they turned my offer down. .-)

I have never given them a single cent. They can get lost!

But of course, this made it impossible for me to own anything in Norway, and in effect I was forced to emigrate in order to be able to own anything. In order to be able to even have a legal income. Mind you, this was not the sole or even main reason I left Norway, but yeah, it contributed. Soviet Norway can be without even my tax money now. They harvest what they sowed.

Let me make it perfectly clear again: every single guy in Norway (other than me) convicted for having set fire to a church were convicted solely because *they confessed*. Yes, they ratted each other out, in their feverish attempts to pin crimes on me, but even that would not have made any difference: the fact that some metal clown tells the police that: "He did it, bruh, I know, I do. **Euronymous** told me so", is not going to hold up in court. They were convicted because they confessed. There was no other (real) evidence! Period.

Yes, I never confessed. There is zero real evidence suggesting I burnt a single church. If you think I actually did, I am fine with that. Please do. I don´t care. But don´t f***ing convict me when you have zero evidence, save some confessions by manipulated morons.

And in a sense they are right to blame me, because **Euronymous** told them I had done it, and pressured them to do the same, because of what I presumably had done. Indirectly, it is in a sense my fault. "I" made them do it. I was the reason they did it.

That is: they really wanted to be accepted as "true" by **Euronymous**, so they did it because of that.

And note: **Immortal** burnt no churches. **DarkThrone** burnt no churches. They were already accepted as "true", so why would they?

Burzum too was accepted as true, of course, not least because **Burzum** was on his own label. But let us keep talking about the others first here.

Hades was not seen as "true". **Emperor** was seen as an **Immortal**-clone. **Enslaved** was seen as a **Burzum**-clone musically, but at least they managed to come up with their own concept, and did not rip-off that from others. They had their own "Viking" theme. That *was* real Black Metal: original, different and at the time fairly unique.

The obvious fact that appears here is that **Burzum** at least would not *need* to burn any churches. **Burzum** was already "true".

11

The truth is more complex than this, though, and I should talk more about this. Yes, people burnt churches because they wanted recognition from **Euronymous**. But there is more to it. We should not deprive these guys of their nobler and deeper motives. One motive does not rule out another, and it is possible to have more than one thought in the head at the same time, you (should...) know.

Let us first start at the beginning. The first attack on Christianity by this scene. I happen to know that originally many individual in the scene were supposed to carry out coordinated attacks on the church in Norway. That is, they were all supposed to burn churches at the same time all over Norway. On June the 6th 1992. On what some believe to be the 1199th anniversary of the (Norwegian) Viking attack on Lindisfarne in England, the main missionary center whence Norway was Christianized. (Why not instead on the 1200th anniversary? I guess, waiting a full year for that was out of the question.)

When the day came, only one single church was burned down. Fantoft stave church. So everyone, save one single individual, failed. Miserably. **Euronymous** said he had not had the time, and instead went out to spray paint anti-Christian slogans in Oslo, on that same day. Another guy claimed he had forgotten all about it, because he was too drunk. The list of excuses was long. But one thing is clear: all save one *failed*.

Now, of course, we don´t know who burnt down the Fantoft stave church, so I will not dwell any more on that, but we also know that **Euronymous** and the others involved in this "coordinated" attack *assumed* that I had done it. We also know that this sat presidency for the rest of the scene, and that **Euronymous** used this to promote more church burnings.

Now, since everyone in the scene *believed* I had done it, thanks to the rumors spread by **Euronymous**, they also blamed me later on for "making" them do the same. To prove that they too were "true".

This was certainly used by them to justify putting the blame on me. To include me in their confessions.

And this next point is important: nobody I ever met in the scene had any problems with burning down churches. In fact, they all found it justified, even cool, and saw it as an act of defense of our Scandinavian heritage. Or in fact, of our Norwegian heritage (and I say that, because nationalism was widespread in our scene).

So yeah, **Euronymous** used this to keep people away from playing Black Metal, because it required a huge amounts of courage, and contempt for the law and public property, to be accepted as "true", but of course there was more to it to the guys who actually burnt the churches. They *wanted* to attack that disgusting institution. They *wanted* to express their contempt for Christianity by burning down these churches!

Everyone in the scene were openly racist and nationalistic, save one single individual: **Euronymous**. Even the only other **Mayhem** member at the time, **Hellhammer**, walked around with a "White Power" button on his jacket, and was openly and strongly anti-immigration. He even put a large German WWII flag on the wall in their rehearsal place! (And when asked about it by journalists in 1993, assured them that I had put that flag there....)

Euronymous on the other hand, we found out after some time, was a Communist. He supported Enver Hoxha and Pol Pot, and their only real tour with **Mayhem** had been in the former DDR. He walked around with a (tiny) Hammer and Sickle symbol on his jacket, and had a huge DDR flag on the wall in his office. He had a deal with the local "Antifa" punks, for protection of his shop, and was politically at odds with *everyone else* in the scene!

Hellhammer obviously knew this already, but the rest of us did not know about it from the start. It was problematic, but personally I had already signed to his label when I found out, and was therefore too involved with his record company to care. Besides, he toned his views down a lot, and did nothing to stop me and others from promoting racism and nationalism in the scene. In fact, we even managed to get him to do the same, for some time. I cannot tell just how much this mattered for him in our later conflict, but I know that I disliked him for his views, and also used this against him once we fell out with each other. Some also claim (and even back then claimed) that he was not actually a Communist, but just pretended to be to provoke. It was easy for us to accept that claim, to justify having anything to do with him.

Before we continue: yes, I talk about **Euronymous** and **Hellhammer** only, when I talk about **Mayhem** and the Norwegian Black Metal scene, because **Necrobutcher** was simply not a part of that scene anymore. Nor were any of the former members of **Mayhem** (I have never met any of them). As **Euronymous** said it: **Necrobutcher** was just "smoking pot with his girlfriend", and did not re-appear in the scene until after **Euronymous** was dead. And *because* he was dead....

Now, do not take this as an insult to **Necrobutcher**. He was furious on **Euronymous** after he had desecrated the remains of **Dead**, after he had committed suicide, so he was not present *because of* **Euronymous**. He has even spoken publicly about how he contemplated killing **Euronymous** himself. It was probably the fact that I killed **Euronymous** that brought **Necrobutcher** back!

Back to the topic of burning churches: the contempt for what was seen as an immigrant cult was total in our scene, as it had been in the Death Metal scene before. At the time, the churches allowed in and protected illegal Afro-Asian immigrants, by letting them live in the churches themselves, giving them "church asylum", so that the police could not get to them and evict them from Norway. As I have already said, with the exception of **Euronymous**, every single individual I met in that scene was anti-immigration, and everyone of them was furious at the damn Christians who protected these illegal immigrants. This made it easy for all of us to not only justify burning their churches down, but also to celebrate it when others did. Openly, the guys I talked to, even hoped that a church *with* immigrants inside would be burnt down one time.

So no, the guys burning churches were not only manipulated to do it, by Euronymous, but did it of their own free will and with an anti-Christian and anti-immigration motive.

Now, when you understand that, you should review the fact that **Euronymous**, when I was arrested in January 1993, went out in public, wearing a white sweater, and apologized on behalf of the entire Black Metal scene, for the "discomfort" we had caused. People in the scene were furious at him! Not only did he prove that he was a coward, but also he undermined all they had done and believed in!

And with what right?

Now, it is true that **Euronymous** too was included in a confession, by **Bard**, who confessed to having set fire to Holmenkollen chapel along with him (and he claimed, also with me), and **Euronymous** always made sure to say that "we" had burnt down another church, to include himself in this as much as possible, but most people who actually knew what was going on, when he did that interview, knew that that he had no right to even speak about it!

12

Between mid 1991 and early 1993, from age 18 to 20, (whilst **Euronymous** was from age 24 to 26, by the way), I made and recorded four full length albums and mini-album, as well as music for at least one more full length album. You could argue that I was in a very productive period of my life.

I would argue that I was in a very destructive period of my life, with very little hope for a future and very few and far between plans for life, and that I just made music because I had nothing better to do.

The fall of the Berlin wall in 1989 made things even worse, because it even took away all hopes I had for a WWIII, a conflict between NATO and the Warsaw Pact – where I could at least have participated (as a partisan in Norway, fighting against both NATO and the Warsaw Pact) and die happily in a storm of steel and fire, wearing my authentic German SS steel helmet (that the police stole from me, when I was arrested in 1993). After 1989, I did not even have that hope left. I was not overly optimistic or positive about life, so to speak.

I can add that yeah, the dynamite, rifles, shotguns and ammo, that the police found in my home when they arrested me, was something I had for this purpose.

By and large, I was completely disinterested in society, and simply did not want to participate in any way. My view was that the good guys had already lost the war, and we were living in the shit that had come after because of that, and all it deserved was to burn, crash and die.

When it came to religion, I grew up, like most Norwegians, with contempt for what we saw as a worthless Christian death cult, and like most other Norwegians I knew perfectly well that Christianity was an immigrant religion, just like Islam is today. I was strongly anti-Christian, and had been since I could walk upright.

My parents where atheists, but also openly anti-Christian. They never baptized my brother and me, and also both left the state church early in life. (I may add that all Norwegians were automatically included in the state church, at birth... a clever way to make Norway look "Christian", I guess). My mother revolted against it even as a child, and said things like: "Mary was just a whore. She did not even know the name of the father of her child." My dad too grew up with parents who had both left the state church. Both my parents were baptized, though.

Racism was also commonplace, both at home and amongst friends. I grew up with family proverbs like: "Never trust anyone with brown eyes", and when I married later in life, my mother was so relieved that I had found one with blue eyes. She had always been so worried that I should marry a woman with brown eyes. She did *not* want grand children with brown eyes! My father also had his opinions, and could say things like: "Everybody who knows history *hates* Jews," suggesting they had all the right in the world to hate them.

Now, this might be shocking to some, but by and large, my situation in relation to racism and religion was not special at all in Norway. I would argue that most Norwegian families were and are like mine was: atheistic and even anti-Christian, racist and sometimes also even directly anti-Jewish.

There is a reason why the ordinary Norwegian police arrested the (few) Jews in Norway during WWII, *on their own initiative* and without the Germans even knowing about it (as much as half of the policemen in Norway at the time were themselves members of *Nasjonal Samling*; the Norwegian NS party), and handed them over to the Germans, who asked: "What are we supposed to do with them?" "Just get them the Hell out of Norway. We don´t want them here".

The system in Norway, the educational system and the authorities, is another story, though.... The Norwegian people and society as a whole is still held under the yoke of Christianity, with all that entails. And Norwegians by and large have learnt to pretend: to say "yes, sure" to the authorities, and then ignore them and do what they want privately. In fact, often Norwegians intentionally do the opposite of what the authorities tell them to.

Now, this makes matters worse, in a sense, because it feels so much extra unfair and unreasonable. Why are a majority of the population, who cares no whit about that immigrant cult, accepting this hostage situation? Why do we let the minority hold us hostage to their ignorant BS? Why must we walk around pretending (and yeah: many in Norway do) to be positive to "Christianity"? Why can we not just take that whole death cult and throw it in the bin, like we should, and return to reason, to our own heritage, to science, to our own roots, and our own culture instead? That desert cult has literally nothing to do with us or our heritage! It is only holding us back, reducing our quality, mixing us up with foreign breeds and helping replacing everything we hold dear in our own homelands. Even our own people, in the end.

Was I "Pagan", though?

Well, sort of, but not really. I knew too little about it to be able to identify directly as "Pagan", but of course, "Paganism" is indeed my heritage. My roots, heritage, my blood, is "Pagan" to the core. I grew up in Odinsvei ("Odin´s Way"), surrounded by other streets named after Frigg, Freyr, Freyja, Baldur, Thrymr, Sleipnir, etc. We all knew perfectly well that *this* was our real heritage. We just did not know enough about it to declare ourselves "Pagans".

And I may ask: whose fault was that, if not the Christians and the people who still clung to Christianity?

Instead of identifying as "Pagans", we – the guys in the Norwegian Black Metal scene – identified mainly as "anti-Christians", and although we rejected nonsense like "The Church of Satan", we often did use Satanic symbols and imagery, to express our contempt for Christianity. There was never any more to it than that, though. No "Satanic rites" or actual "Satanism". Sometimes we pretended that this existed, again to provoke and express contempt for Christianity, and to keep "posers" away, but no. It did not exist. In spite of what has been said, there was not one single individual in that scene who was actually a "Satanist". Even **Euronymous**, who pretended to be, was just saying that to provoke.

Where there bad and immoral people there? Yes! Indeed.

But mainly, I think, we can say that the people in that scene were disillusioned. Lost in a world of lies. Uprooted (by Christianity) and feeling that they were denied a meaningful existence.

Personally, as I have said many times already, I played music only because I had nothing better to do, and what I really wanted was to join the guys who fought and died during WWII, in the fight against Capitalism and Bolshevism. Even dying for an already lost cause had more meaning to me than living for what came after that. But I had been denied the opportunity to do even that. There no longer was any such army to join. And after 1989 even the hope for a WWIII was lost.

To many of us, starting a war of our own instead, in Norway, against the cause of our problems, made sense.

"The Count", trying to look like an undead creature.

13

With time the purity spiraling of **Euronymous** took even more extreme forms, and he made up a lie about how the Black Metal scene was really a type of organization, with him in the leading role, of course, that he called "The Inner Circle", some sort of Black Metal mafia. Sadly, we – the others – played along for some time, and pretended that there was such a thing, but it was all nonsense. So no, there never was any "Inner Circle", other than in his mind and in lies.

My debut album, released in March 1992, recorded in January the same year. Notice the Burzum name being in very poor resolution. I called the image "A Lost Forgotten Sad Spirit".

14

One of the most common questions I get from Black Metal fans is: "What instrument did you use for this or that track or this or that album?"

Yeah, I know: some people care about such things, and I know some people in the Norwegian black metal scene too cared about such things, **Euronymous** included. But I never did.

From the start, I had that same (pearl white **Weston**) guitar, and I was perfectly happy with it. Other musicians were interested in their instruments, but I could not care less, as long as it worked. And it did.

I have no idea beyond that. Yeah, I used a **Marshal** amp for one guitar track on the debut album, and I regretted having used it ever since. For most of the others I used my 60 watts **Peavey** amp, and I found that to be perfect for what I wanted. For the **Filosofem** album I used my brother´s stereo amp, to get a sound as similar as possible to the sound I had in my headset at home, when playing and making my music.

When it comes to drums, bass guitar, synths and microphones for the vocals... I used whatever I had, or in the case of **Filosofem**, I used a headset as a microphone.

Although some instruments are clearly of better quality than others, I think by and large that what matters is what you do with them. How you play. What you play. Why you play...

If you want to play original and *real* Black Metal, use whatever gives you your own unique sound. That is all.

15

Some have described me as being some sort of outsider in the Black Metal scene, and not really a metal head, and I would argue that this is correct. Sure, I too had listened to some metal music in my life, but I was never really a metal head. Concerts were not my thing (and I know, because I went to a few), the whole metal-look was not my thing and my musical roots stretched back into classical music a lot more than any metal music. Nor did I drink, I may add. Nor did I appreciate the cheap and drunken rock and roll culture of most metal heads.

The odd claim that **Euronymous** and me were competing for the leader role of that metal music scene is as ridicules as it sounds. Not only was I an outsider from the start, coming from a completely different background, I more and more not only wanted to leave that scene behind, but also actually took steps to leave it.

Yeah, I know **Euronymous** saw me as competition, and as a challenger to his leading role, but that was a pure projection on his behalf: I had no interest whatsoever in being "the leader" of that scene. And everything I have done since proves that. I distanced myself from that scene as much as I could, as early as in 1993, but more and more after that.

Later, with Black Metal turned into a parody of what **Euronymous** outwards wanted it to be (in reality he just wanted other bands to stay away....), I certainly did not want to be associated with it!

What I saw was the rise of a MSM-created genre, only loosely based on what we created in 1991 and 1992. I saw what not only I, but even, and I think especially, **Euronymous** would have utterly disliked.

Further, I saw the original Black Metal guys assimilate into this MSM created parody of Black Metal, as if everything about it was fine. **Immortal** turning into a mobile circus of clowns, **Mayhem** turning into classical rock and roll stars, the wanna-be hang-around bands, like **Emperor** and **Enslaved**, and even **Satyricon**, turning into "trve kvlt original Black Metals bands, bruh". Even **Fenris** of **DarkThrone** cooperated with these guys, although I think we could argue that **DarkThrone** compromised itself the least of them all.

No. Sorry. I do not want anything to do with this. And that has been my attitude since 1994.

I write about it now to have some sort of closure. To hammer into stone the fact that this is *not* what Black Metal was supposed to be.

And from a human point of view, it is sad to see how people are so willing to sell out, the moment they can. This is also important to stress: these bands were underground because they were new and/or kind of bad. I am sure that had they been given the opportunity to sell out earlier, they would have. They did at first opportunity.

Ok. I guess that is what mankind is like. And I am not happy with it. Most people are not *Menschen*, but *Untermenschen*.

All movements seem to be like that. We saw it extremely vividly with the Hippie movement, where these former "peace and love" people turned into the most vile, hateful and rotten Capitalist pigs and professional liars this world has ever seen, but we see it pretty much everywhere else too.

Idealists are almost always only such because they have to be. They have no other options, and once they get more options, they cast aside their ideals like were they wet towels.

And no, I am not completely immune to this myself. I am not saying that. But this is an observation I have made, and that I wish to share here. And this is an observation that should make most people see the whole Black Metal scene and what came after, in a different light.

16

The idea of using corpse paint surely came from earlier heavy metal and even rock and roll bands, such as **Alice Cooper**. It was of course used differently in our scene, not to look cool, but to look.... dead. "Anti-sexy". But I think we can agree that the idea came from **Alice Cooper**.

You could argue that it made sense, to use corpse paint in Black Metal, for several reasons. It was anti-trend, because not one single Death Metal band used it. It was seen by them seen as cringe, old-fashioned and even for posers (because some of the older heavy metal bands had done it). It was also anti- the idea of becoming famous, because you basically hid your real identify, behind a mask. And I may add: you also did that whilst using a pseudonym, instead of your real name.

Although we can all agree that I failed miserably in this, I was motivated by this myself, the wish to stay anonymous, and I was inspired by white label underground techno/house bands, who also kept their real identifies completely "secret". Their albums were even released with only a white label on them. No artist names. No track lists. Nothing. I liked that idea. Nobody knew who had actually made the music.

Immortal wanted to basically become the new **Kiss**, so to them it meant something completely different, and I am sure others in the scene had other motives too, some good and others cringe. So I cannot really speak for them, because there was no consensus on this.

In hindsight I think it was interesting from a more Pagan perspective, because by rejecting Christianity we tried to bring back the spirit of our Pagan ancestors. In our heritage, in order to see a ghost, a spirit, an elf, you need to actually wear a mask. And corpse paint is such a mask. You could say that by putting on such a mask, we could relate more directly to our distant ancestors and their wishes. We could receive their influence more readily.

But yeah: by and large, it was just an anti-Death Metal thing to do, and it became popular.

17

Some British metal magazines started claiming that Black Metal was a British invention, and that **Venom** was the first Black metal band, but this just shows that they have no idea what Black Metal was to begin with. Yes, the name was taken from a **Venom** album, but that album was not Black Metal. **Venom** was a Thrash Metal band, or perhaps just a Heavy Metal band. Black Metal as a music genre did not exist back then. The name was picked by **Euronymous**, and the only reason why he picked that name was because he thought it sounded cool, and unlike most of the others in that scene, actually pretended to like **Venom**.

Their next level of cope is to call the Norwegian Black Metal for "second wave Black Metal", in an attempt to claim that their British **Venom** was the original.

As one of the guys in the Norwegian Black Metal scene from 1991 to 1993, I can tell that I had barely even heard about **Venom** in 1991, and I have yet to meet anyone in that scene who actually listened to **Venom** or even claimed to like it or have ever liked it, save **Euronymous**. And even he never listened to it. He just claimed (pretended?) to like it. And why would he like it? **Venom** is garbage.

Further, I can point at the fact that Venom did not come up with the name "Black Metal" themselves either. The term was apparently first used by a German metal band called **Holy Moses**, on their demo tape called **Black Metal Masters**, from 1980...

I have never seen any British metal magazines claim that *they* were the first Black Metal band, though...

My second album, Det som engang var ("What once was"), with artwork based on an AD&D module.

18

I only met **Dead** once, and barely talked to him. Other than sharing a meal with him, I once walked with him to a local shop, and back again to their home, and we did not speak a lot. I do not remember much what we spoke about.

As a curiosity, I can tell that later on **Euronymous** told me that **Dead** had been horrified by the fact that one of the guys from Bergen, **Padden** from **Old Funeral**, had not even heard about **Venom**. At the time, mid-to-late 1992, I could correct **Euronymous** and tell him that he had mistaken **Padden** for me, because I was the one who had told **Dead** that I had not even heard about **Venom**.

Interestingly, had **Euronymous** known that at the time, he would probably not have signed **Burzum** to his label at all.

As I have explained before, in this book, this kind of purity spiraling was common. If you had not listened to "this or that band" since at least 1984, you were not "true". This would of course have been impossible for younger musicians, because they would have been too young back then anyhow, to listen to anything at all, so it was just a petty way to make sure that only "you" were special and important. "The others?! LOL! They are not veterans like me!"

As a result we saw a whole lot of metal kids lie about what bands they had listened too, and correspondingly, we made fun of these guys, saying things like "I have listened to **Venom** since I was an egg in my mother´s womb, dude!".

So if you really, really want to be a trve kvlt Black Metal guy, but you are 13 years old in 2024, you might feel relief when I tell you that it is okay for you not to have listened to some crappy Thrash (or Trash...) Metal band since the 80ies...

Finally, in this context, I can add that I actually had heard about **Venom**, but had forgotten all about it when asked about it by **Dead**. A friend of mine had satellite TV in the 80ies, and his big brother was watching TV in the background, and almost laughed his heart out when **Venom** performed live on his TV (probably on a show called "**Headbangers Ball**"). They were so bad that they were just a joke to him. I was there that day. That was my entire **Venom** experience until **Dead** asked me about them, in early 1991...

Note also that it was not about having listened to older Black Metal, because that was a new term. The point was to prove that you were not a newcomer, and that you had listened to Thrash and Heavy Metal a long time already! **Bathory**? **Venom**? Sure, but also other bands that has since then not been identified as having anything to do with Black Metal at all. Early **Kreator**. **Destruction**. I think even **Metallica**.

The guys in **Emperor** also listened to **King Diamond** and **Merciful Fate** and that kind of music. **Immortal** was basically obsessed with **Kiss** and their stage shows. I am sure some guys in the scene had listened to **Alice Cooper** – and **Scorpions** too for that sake, although when I say that, this is purely speculations on my part.

Nobody ever claimed **King Diamond**, **Merciful Fate** or **Kiss** were the "first wave" of Black Metal bands because of that, though...

19

The "problem" with music that becomes popular is that... it becomes popular. So there is no holding it back. In reality, there is of course no reason to either, but as I have explained here, **Euronymous** and the rest of us too, saw a reason to hold it back. We had different reasons, but we all saw a reason to hold it back.

At best, we just wanted to avoid making the mistakes that we had seen Death Metal bands make. We did not want all the bands to sound the same!

Euronymous, as I have explained, just wanted to make sure that his own band became the biggest and most famous, and that before any others had the time to become influential and important.

Honestly, all these views were legit, and understandable, in a world of competition, but at the same time, it made no sense. Other bands are in reality not your *competitor*. And if a band becomes bigger and more famous than your own... so what? Especially, why care if your band becomes big and famous as well? Are you really that envious and petty? Come on!

Also, if you make music that others like, then of course they will emulate your style, and make music that sounds much like your music. Don´t see it, like we did (!), as theft! See it as a compliment! They just prove that your music is awesome, by making more in the same style. By "stealing" your ideas.

Our problem was that we built our whole concept around *not* stealing from others, around being *original*. So it became hard not to react negatively when others started "stealing" ideas and making "un-original" music. In effect, the Black Metal style was dead the moment it became popular.

Note also that it was **DarkThrone**, **Burzum** and **Immortal** who became popular, who made this scene musically, and the others emulated their styles. This became therefore identified as Black Metal. *That* was how Black Metal was supposed to sound. Or so people thought... and so it became.

Had other bands, inspired by other bands, become popular before these three or instead of them, then the idea of what Black Metal is supposed to sound like would have been completely different!

And yeah, I may sound like a prick sometimes, when I talk about this, but I live under no illusions, and have a very relaxed relationship to this. I do not see

Enslaved and **Emperor**, or other today famous "Black Metal" bands, as thieves of our style. Instead I do take it as a compliment, because I understand that they simply were inspired by us, and did much the same for that reason, and that our ideas of Black Metal were flawed to begin with. I am even perfectly open to the idea that their music is better than my own, or than that of **DarkThrone** or **Immortal**. In fact, I am pretty sure a lot of Black Metal that came after is indeed better than anything I ever made. And that is just fine. I am sure **Burzum** will still be appreciated by many anyhow, so why should I care?

When I do not talk about **Mayhem** in this context, that is because they only had one single cool track (**Freezing Moon**) out throughout this period, from 1991 to 1993, and therefore (sadly?) had very little musical influence on the scene, on the bands that came after. As you certainly have understood by now, this was also one of the things that frustrated **Euronymous**: his band was kind of insignificant in all of this.

I am not saying **Mayhem** *is* insignificant, but at the time it was, *musically*. I am sure it became also a major musical influence on the genre later on.

20

After **Euronymous** had hyped my name (i. e. my pseudonym, "The Count") so much in the scene, after he released my debut album on his label, he realized that I was seen as the most extreme musician in all the scene, so...

... what would make more sense than to ask me if I could play the bass lines for the **Mayhem** album? That way **Mayhem** would still be seen as the most extreme band... He had no contact with **Necrobutcher** after all, so he was basically not in the band anymore anyhow.

I failed to see his true motives, and agreed to play the bass on their album, in studio in September 1992. We rehearsed sometimes (not many....) in Oslo, and then recorded the album.

During the recording I tried not to interfere too much with the mixing, because I was just a studio musician, and I respectfully wanted them to get the sound they wanted. Their own unique style! So I actually just recorded the bass lines and left...

But this was also just seen as a betrayal by him. In his eyes, I just showed a total lack of interest in his music. He felt insulted.

So many things to argue meaninglessly about in this world... right?

I would like to add that I was always very impressed with the drumming of **Hellhammer**, who basically carried the whole album with his drumming. Without him, **Mayhem** would have been nothing.

And since we are on the topic: yes, it is true that I made several of the bass lines played on that album, and also that I was not credited with having either played on the album or made some of the music. That is fine, though. I never cared. **Hellhammer** did that do get **Euronymous´** parents off his back.

21

Whenever I hear about my case, I learn that Varg "killed his friend, bruh". As you can tell from this book, we were certainly not friends. We were at best for a very brief time band mates and most of the time just business associates: he ran the label releasing my album. I had more to do with him than would have been normal in that situation mainly because he was utterly incompetent, and ran his business into the ground. Since my own band depended on his business success, I tried to do something about that, as I have explained elsewhere in this book.

So no. I never killed "my friend", as some have suggested. I killed a former business associate, whom I most of the time strongly disliked, and who probably most of the time strongly disliked me. Note also that we lived 310+ miles apart, and therefore obviously had very little to do with each other, most of the time. The vast majority of our communication was via phone. When some try to depict it as if we were friends who normally socialized, this is simply not true. I never "partied" with any of the guys in the Oslo area, or even had common friends with them.

And no, even though I liked both **Fenris**

and **Hellhammer**, I rarely met them and would not even consider them as former friends. Just guys I knew somewhat. Music contacts. Acquaintances. My *friends* lived in my home town Bergen. I never killed any of them...

My girlfriend too lived in Bergen, and I can add that when she became pregnant with my child, **Euronymous** sat in his shop in Oslo telling people that I should punch her in the stomach to provoke an abortion, because he hated children, he said. He also claimed that he had never been a child himself.

My *best* friend, Jarle, from childhood, died from an overdose many years ago. He never met **Euronymous**, and would not even have known he had ever existed had I not killed him.

My girlfriend at the time only briefly met **Euronymous** once, in Bergen, when he was there in relation to some studio recording.

I never met his (former?) girlfriend, and saw her for the first time when she testified in court in 1994, after I had killed him.

Contrary to what some claim, there never were any "girl problems" in this scene. Not between anyone, from what I know. Never. No jealousy. Nothing.

22

So I talk about how **Immortal** wanted to become the new **Kiss**, and others who aimed to become big and important bands (as if a band can be "important"....), but what about me? Had I no grand plans for **Burzum**?

Initially, and for a long time, I just played music because I had nothing better to do. I did not dream about fame or holding concerts. When I joined **Old Funeral**, I was kind of forced to play live, because they wanted to, and my conclusion was that this was not something I liked or wanted to do more. I was only happy to leave and form my own solo-band, **Burzum**, where I could control everything and do whatever I wanted to. And avoid playing live...

My ambition was to release albums. Not to play concerts. Not to become recognized by passersby, when out in the public. So yeah, I was not the typical metal head.

However, in 1992, I did flirt with the idea of playing live, mainly because I was asked a lot about it, and for some time I looked for other musicians to do it with, but....

Nah.

It took forever to teach them even the simplest riffs, and perhaps worst of all: I had to relate to other musicians again (a special kind of obnoxious breed, I have to say, almost as bad as people who call themselves "artists").

I quickly abandoned that idea, and walked away from it, and I have never looked back.

If you will, I can explain how **Burzum** was intended, by me. First of all, when I produced the albums, the microphones for the drums were set up so that when you put on a headset and started listening to it, you would hear it from the perspective of the musician playing the music. Mainly from the perspective of the drummer. You *were* that musician, in a sense, playing the music, when you listened to it.

Naturally, this would work less well at a concert, where you would get an inverted sound picture presented to you.

Yes, **Burzum** was made by me, but also first and foremost for me. I wanted to listen to it, and I wanted that the way I heard it when I made it.

This is how I imagined **Burzum** being listened to as well: in solitude, on a walkman or on a normal stereo with a headset. Or indeed in the car.

So in a sense I did not fit in here, in any metal scene. I was not your typical metal head, for sure, dreaming of becoming a guitar hero on some stage. I have never been envious of those bands who picked the classical rock and roll route, and started touring and playing live. On the contrary, I felt that I had dodged a bullet there.

Me as a 5 year-old, with my dad´s knife in a belt.

23

The artwork for my albums was at first intended to come in pairs, in the sense that one cover would fit perfectly with the other. So my debut album cover was actually only a small part of what I planned for the second album. Since I had this fantasy concept for the band, because I liked fantasy, missed the time when I played role-playing games and wanted to have something different from the others, the cover artwork was heavily inspired by an adventure module (**The Temple of Elemental Evil**) for **Advanced Dungeons & Dragons**. For copyright reasons, I asked a girl in Bergen to draw something similar, instead of trying to use that image itself. I intentionally opted for black and white cover art, because that would cost less to print.

The second cover was more of the same, and by the time I made the third and fourth album, I had decided to use Theodor Kittelsen (a famous Norwegian artist) images for both those covers. For the first one, again, I opted for the cheap black and white artwork, but by the time I made the cover for the fourth album, **Filosofem**, I had a record company in England releasing my records, and they would cover the printing costs (i. e. not pay me royalties until those expenses had been covered), so I used an image in colors for that one.

The first Kittelsen image was from his "the black death" series, and was used because it fitted the concept of the album, **Hvis Lyset tar oss,** dealing with how Christianity is a spiritual black death.

The second Kittelsen image was used, I think in 1993 or 1994, for **Filosofem**, because it was in the same style, and because it was totally... anti-Black Metal. As I have stated elsewhere in this book, I really felt a need to distance myself from the by then "ruined" Black Metal scene.

The idea that Black Metal covers had to be in black and white is because of this. In reality, this was the case only because we had very little money and had to pick the cheapest option...

The cover art for the mini-album, called **Aske** ("Ash" or "Ashes") was just a (black and white...) photograph of the burnt-out ruins of Fantoft stave church. The photograph was taken by a friend of mine from that time, **Are**. He was originally (and also) a friend of **Harald**, that I got to know through him.

24

From 1991 to 1993 there was no drug abuse in the scene, save some pot smokers here and there, but most of the guys drank heavily. Some of them so much that they would have been defined as alcoholics by any sane society.

Personally, I did not even drink alcohol, or smoked cigarettes, but I was an anomaly in that sense. Or if you like: also in that sense...

From what I have heard, this changed later on, but that would be outside the scope of this book. I write about what was between 1991 and 1993, not what came later, when I was no longer a part of this.

I am not surprised by hearing about that, though. The whole music industry is rotten to the core, completely degenerate, soiling anyone who comes into contact with it, and with that I have yet another argument not get involved with it. The less you have to do with it, the better.

25

One of the things I did differently, was to write lyrics in Norwegian. Also, the band name itself, **Burzum**, was picked intentionally, in order *not* to sound "cool" in English. This was a result of my "nationalist" and anti-American attitudes, where I instead wanted to promote my own heritage (here; language) and reject the Americanization that I so vividly saw happening all around me.

Burzum itself, though, was in a fantasy language, from **Tolkien´s** universe, and it means "Darkness". It was taken from the little poem written on the One Ring in **The Lord of the Rings**. The part: "agh burzum ishi-krimpatul", meaning "and in the darkness bind you."

This was something I had come into contact with via role-playing games, around age 12 or 13, in particular **MERP, Middle-earth Role-playing**, that inspired me to read the books as well, starting with **The Hobbit,** before I continued to **The Lord of the Rings**.

And yeah: that was my "special theme" for **Burzum**: fantasy.

In the **Spell of Destruction** lyrics, from the debut album, you can also clearly see some Lovecraftian influence, with the made-up words in the "spell" that is cast there. This was more from the **Call of Cthulhu** role-playing game, based on H. P. Lovecraft stories, rather than from his stories, though.

Hvis Lyset tar oss ("If the Light takes us"), an album where Christianity is imagined as a spiritual Black Death presenting itself as "light" and where sanity and health is called "darkness". Recorded the Summer of 1992.

26

Some has asked me if I had any musical training, and whenever someone asks me this, I always stress that if I had any formal training in this context, I would probably not have been able to make any music at all. Or if I had been able to, it would not have been any different from other music in any way. Formal education *removes* originality, different ways to look at things and basically ruins your ability to make original music. You learn how to play well, but you learn how to play just like everybody else do it. Now, I am sure such an education is very useful, in fact even necessary, if you want to play in some orchestra or something like that, but for a composer who intends to *make music* for a living? Nah. (I might be wrong here, though.)

Even in the metal scene, people often claimed I held my plectrum the "wrong" way, if they saw me playing the guitars, because they had been conditioned into thinking there was a "right and wrong" in music. When simply answered them that: "This is how I hold the plectrum", they were visibly troubled by it. It might not come as a surprise to you, if I tell you that I never heard any music ever made by any of these guys. They probably all claim they are better guitar players than I ever was, though...

The truth is that **Burzum** was indeed fairly original. Not everything was, and you can see clear influences there from "un-typical" genres, in this context. I was influenced more by classical music than by other metal, and more by Balalaika than by other metal bands, when it came to how I played the guitars.

And there is nothing wrong with that, of course. I did nothing wrong here... I just played music in a different way. And mixed it in a different way too. I specifically asked the sound technician for a more dynamic sound, exactly like they do for classical music recordings, instead of the more statically loud sound of metal productions.

Also, I included non-metal music, from the first album and onwards! Not just as "intros" or "outros" or as a background sound effect, but as actual tracks. Nobody else that I know of did that at the time.

Now, nothing of this was particularly revolutionary, when it came to music production, but it did make **Burzum** into something with a peculiar sound, and that was my objective after all.

I can add that I am not under the impression that I did such a great job, making music, but at least some people like it, and I am perfectly okay with the fact that most people probably don´t. Each to his own.

I like it. So... who cares what others think?

27

Personally I started listening to **Iron Maiden** when I was around 12. I later started listening to **Slayer**, early **Kreator** and also **Bathory´**s **Blood. Fire. Death** album. I never liked **Metallica**, **Megadeth**, **Sodom** or in fact most other thrash metal bands, and yeah, I had in fact some albums from bands I did not really appreciate, like **Voivod**, **Celtic Frost** and a few others. These were just albums I had purchased pre-1989, *hoping* they were good – and I was disappointed. I was also familiar, via my friend Karl (r. i. p.) with e. g. **Ozzy Osbourne**, and I think also **Accept**, but this was never my cup of tea. (Although **Princess of the Dawn** is pretty good!) I also had one **Destruction** album, **Infernal Overkill**, that I really liked.

Other than that, I really did not listen to any metal music. My friend Anders (r. i. p.) introduced me to **The Cure**, but even though I liked it, I never had any of their albums, until long into the 2000s. I was also exposed to the horrors of normal pop music at home, as my older brother listened to that... crap. He also listened to **Marillion**, which had some good tracks, I think, and **Iron Maiden**.

As I have said before, I had never even heard about the term Death Metal until I met the guys in **Amputation** and **Old Funeral**, in 1989.

On a side note, since it has been brought up by some, I can tell that no, I never listened to **Scorpions**. And I never wore any patches for any bands on my clothes. Ever. So... nah.

I was very fond of underground house and techno music, especially white label, and often went to a club in Bergen, the club **Fønix**, where they played this real loud.

When I after the media rush in January 1993 wanted to relax, I went to that place. It was a very effective means to get rid of metal head followers, for sure. They *hated* that type of music...

I would just stand there, into the early hours, listening to house and techno music, and then go home to play the guitars. Inspired.

Yeah, I had "followers" at the time. Fan boys and fan girls who just kept following me, when I went out. I did not appreciate it. My anonymity had not just been lost, because of my attempt to save **Euronymous´** shop with that newspaper interview, but it had even been replaced by fame (or if you like: infamy), and I had become a celebrity in my home town.

Yeah, I think we just touched upon another reason for me moving from Norway to France. I can go out here, without being recognized by everyone. I can be anonymous! Just like I always wanted!

People who have this anonymity should know that they will probably miss it a lot, if they ever lose it. And once it is lost, you can often never get it back. Ever.

No matter how much you miss it.

"My kingdom for a hint of anonymity!"

Filosofem ("Philosopheme"), recorded in March 1993 as an anti-Black Metal album, in protest of the fact that Black Metal had already become a trend.

28

Hell was located in one of the worst areas of Oslo, and not only was it overflowing with immigrants and "Antifa" punks, but also criminals, of all types. The guy who lived above **Hell** (I am talking about the record shop here, in case you wonder....) was a career criminal, and another one lived just outside, around the corner, in a (VW T3) van. He had a building nearby, with truck loads of stolen goods, that he sold.

As I have explained already, for some time I was there, to help out **Euronymous** and the others working there, so that his economy would get back on track and he could afford to print more **Burzum** albums. Unlike him and his friends, I had a car, so I did a lot of driving. And one day I left the shop for an errand I quickly noticed that I was being followed by a car with two guys in it. Naturally, I was not all that familiar with the layout of Oslo, but I knew one way I could take, to make sure if I was actually followed or not. Because why would I be followed in Oslo? It made no sense, after all.

Now, I can add that this was not the first time I had been followed by guys in a car. The last time was when I was 15, and I was driving my moped. A car full of (5) young men followed me in a car, and after some time I was sure they wanted to beat me up or something, because they just kept following me even when I tried to get away, and took all sorts of illogical turns and strange routes. I had modified the engine of my moped, so instead of doing just over 30 mph it was doing close to 60, and they were following me in my home area. So I knew every in an out of the place. Also, I had never seen those guys before, so I did not know any of them. All I knew was that they were following me, and that they were all much older than me.

At the end of Sleipnersvei ("Sleipnir´s Way") a part of the road had these rather abrupt speed bumps, so I turned sharply and accelerated over the speed bumps literally jumping over them with the moped. The car following me did the same, but obviously the driver was not aware of the speed bumps, so I could hear the metallic sound of his car smashing into them and/or the asphalt after the car had driven over them, and I was convinced that this would not make them any less interested in beating me up for sure. At the end of that little road there was a steep turn to the left, leading into a field and a little forested area. The access was really narrow, so I knew they would not be able to follow me there. This was my "get-away" point.

Because I drove way too fast, and because the path leading into the field at first rose a bit, over a tiny hill of dirt, I jumped at least 5-6 meter with my moped, into the field, and landed in mud. I was stuck!

Behind me the lower front of the car dug into the hard-packed dirt, as they basically crashed into it, and because the access was so narrow, the doors on the passenger´s side were completely blocked, so they could not get out of the car that way.

On the driver´s side, both doors opened and two guys came running out, towards me. Their car probably had at least cosmetic damage, if not even more serious damage, and they looked furious! They were all dressed up, in nice clothing, so I figured they had been on their way to a party or something, and the first one out tripped and fell like a wooden board flat on his face into the mud.

The other one did not slip and fall, but looked even more furious now! He quickly got close to me, and was only a few yards behind me when I simply gave full throttle on the moped, and spun up an immense spray of mud – directly onto him, and I literally covered him with mud. Not just on his face or a bit here and there, but from the top of his hair to the bottom of his shoe soles, he was completely brown from mud, so much that he stopped and just stood there for a moment. I probably blinded him completely with the mud. At the same time, I pushed the moped forwards with my feet, "walking it" forwards, and – whilst I kept spraying him with mud – I spun off. I was no longer bogged! I continued over the field and unto another road, on the other side.

I am pretty sure this was one of the most funny things that ever happened in my life. Had this been a scene in a film, it would have been too perfect to be even half-way believable, but it actually happened to me in real life. And I laughed all the way back home – and never saw these guys again, ever. Or indeed their (probably wrecked) car.

To this day, I have no idea what they wanted, or why they followed me, but they for sure were up to no good, and probably learned a thing or two about not following innocent teenagers. .-)

The problem in Oslo was that I really did not know of any such handy escape routes, and besides, I too was driving a car. I drove for some time, and in the end was absolutely sure that I was being followed. So I picked a narrow road where none could drive past me, and a few hundred yards in, I stopped the car. I picked up a large knife that I had in the car (and that I naturally would have preferred a lot to my little "pocket knife" that I used to kill Euronymous with, if I had wanted to kill him that day, but…. by all means remember: "hE plAnNeD to KiLl hIm, BruH"), and I went out. The driver of the other car immediately started to reverse. I started running after them, to catch up with them, and he sped up, but at the end of the road, they turned abruptly and drove off. Back whence we had come.

Strange.

Upon my return to **Hell** I told the guys what had happened, and shortly after the two men entered the shop, identifying themselves as policemen.

Oh, crap. I had, armed with a large knife, chased two policemen down the road…

But they did not even mention it, and simply told us that they had received tips that this place was full of stolen good. So they wanted to look around a bit.

When they found nothing, they said good bye and left.

In reality, the tip they had received was good. The guy living above **Hell** had his entire apartment full of stolen goods as well as drugs, and he lived on the same address – only one flight up. They had followed me, because I had carried something into my car from this address, and I had driven off. So they gave chase.

Naturally, there was no reason for them to confront me when I chased them down the road armed with a knife. The whole situation was their fault! They were the ones not identifying themselves as policemen and following me. I did what any sane man would do: if you cannot get away, confront the pursuers and deal with them. I did by chasing them away. I technically had done nothing wrong.

29

One of the realizations I have had, when I look at everything in hindsight, is that this scene was not really one scene. You had **Hell** and the guys who hung out or even worked there, and then a number of customers to that shop, whom all met the salesman version of **Euronymous**, and in later years always described him as "so friendly and kind." Yeah, he was trying to sell them records, and then he trash talked them the moment they left.

Then you had the Death Metal scene, still somewhat overlapping with the Black Metal scene, with people who kept on playing Death Metal, who disagreed with **Euronymous** and who still sometimes dropped by in his shop to have a chat or buy a record. Old friends of **Euronymous**. Even though I never saw any of them, I know they were there, in 1991 to 1993, but they were never really seen as a part of that particular scene. Perhaps we could say that they were. I don't know.

In Bergen we had **Immortal** and me as well as the guys in **Old Funeral**, who never went to Oslo or talked with **Euronymous** on the phone – and who probably just wanted to keep on doing what they liked to do: play metal music. Period.

In Notodden you had **Thou Shall Suffer** (later **Emperor**) and in the Haugesund area **Enslaved**. We met a few times and also corresponded with each other – and they too went a few times to Oslo and **Hell**, and were certainly under the influence of **Euronymous**.

Fenris worked in a post distribution central in Oslo, and would every day after work buy a case of beer and bring it to drink it in **Hell**, before he took the train home later on (dead drunk...), to a place called Ski. The other guys in **DarkThrone** were pretty much never there.

Speaking of, some metal guys in the Oslo area stayed away from **Hell**, intentionally, because they disliked the development, or because they disliked the people hanging out there.

This was not a large underground movement at all! Or even a very well defined one.

When I had to read through hundreds of interviews with people claiming I had burnt down the Fantoft stave church, that was because these guys were most of them just... customers of his shop. Often guys who only had ordered a record or two from him via phone. Sometimes they were Death Metallers.

Where they a part of this scene? I guess in a sense, yes. They too spoke to **Euronymous**. They too listened to the music. They too were influenced by **Euronymous**, and his ideas. They too often identified as "Black Metallers", I would think.

I am simply wrong if I claim people I never met where not part of the scene that I was a part of. Although I have done before, and am still tempted to do the same.

What I am right to do, though, is to claim that they have no reason to believe that they can know better than me about this scene or the instrumental people in it, as they often seem to do. Their version of events is necessarily not incorrect, per se. This is their perspective. But I know more. I know better. Sadly, I have to say. I was the one who paid the steepest price for the fame/infamy of this movement.

I am not proud of having been part of this movement. The years 1991 to 1993 were characterized by despair, lies, frustration, conflict and hopelessness. In the wake of this, the positive fruits were drowned in a sea of envy, hatred and pettiness. But it is always easy to look back and only then know what you should have done. Hindsight is the most accurate science in the world, but also the most useless.

30

If **Euronymous** was wrong, and it was not because Death Metal musicians started wearing bland clothing and have worried looks on their faces on band photos, then why actually did **Dead** kill himself?

I don´t know.

Your guess is probably as good as mine.

Now, I never "partied" with any of the guys in Oslo, but **Hellhammer** told me that they sometimes did, and one time **Dead** was drunk, he actually stabbed **Euronymous**, with a knife, because of an underlying conflict between them, that I am not qualified to talk about.

He had moved from Sweden to join their band, and was obviously not happy with his situation, that much we can say for sure. They did not even rehearse, and he just sat there, in his room in the house they had rented in the countryside.

Yeah, with that knowledge, your guess is as good as mine.

31

Many ask me why this Black Metal phenomena started in Norway, of all places, but at best I can refer to what I have told you in this book, and perhaps you can decide for yourself based on that.

I guess this combination of events, individuals and contrasting opinions by chance appeared first in Norway.

Why?

I don´t know. Or maybr we Norwegians are just a bit more individualistic and "difficult" than other Germanic peoples? Or untamed, if you like.

What more can I say?

32

My feelings to modern Black Metal are barely there. I have intentionally not paid any attention to it, so I know very little about it. I decided not to be apart of this, starting as early as 1993, even before I killed **Euronymous**, and I never looked back.

And no: even though I have made metal music, also after that, I was never again part of any music scene. And I did not see my music as part of any particular metal genre either.

Later on, from August 1993 an onwards, I had other and more pressing concerns, with the perspective of having to serve 12 years in a prison system run by the same people responsible for the kangaroo court that convicted me.

(Yeah. 21 years in prison back then meant that I would only have to actually serve 12 years,)

Like a guy in Ila prison said it, after his sister had come to visit him, and only talked about whether she should paint the bathroom in pink or white. This troubled her so much, and she could not decide! "I am trying to survive here, and she expects me to worry about that!?"

33

No, I do not miss the Norwegian Black Metal scene, as it was in 1991 to 1992, and into 1993. Nor do I miss the people in that scene, whether they were friends or just acquaintances back then. Not even those who were cool, like **Fenris** and **Hellhammer**. They took one path in life, and I took another.

On a personal level, whether I made a mistake to join the Death Metal underground in 1989 or not, with all that lead to eventually, is irrelevant. This made me into what I am today. This was one of my adventures in life, so to speak, and I gained a lot of XP from it and leveled up many times.

The Black Metal sub-culture that we see today is not a result of our scene, as much as it is a result of how the MSM presented it to the public. This is what always happens, when European youth come up with some new tribal way to revolt against the criminal regimes and the yoke they live under. It happened to the hippie movement, that started out as a very Pagan back-to-the-nature movement, but ended up as a pro-Communist, multicultural, STD-spreading drug-fest, because of the MSM. It happened to punk too. It happened to all movements that sprung up from the people itself. If they cannot suppress it, they take control over it, and use it to keep people in check.

The racism, the ethnic nationalism, the anti-Abrahamism, the Paganism and not least the "activism" of this revolt, the things they were actually worried about, were toned down, rooted out or ignored by the MSM, and Black Metal became to a large degree (but yeah, still not entirely,) a toothless, harmless "Satanic" clown-show, that nobody takes seriously.

All the films and books made about this, by their agents and useful idiots, must be seen in this light. Their infantile slander and their many character murders of me must be seen in this light too, because as history has shown, I am pretty much the only one who were part of this who never danced to their tune, in any way. It makes sense that I am the one they more than anyone else want to destroy publicly. They really do not want anyone to listen to me.

Thank you for being brave enough to read my side of this story.

Good luck to you. *Heill auk Sæll!*

Varg Vikernes
January 2024

Other Books by Varg Vikernes:

***"It is praiseworthy to do what is right,
not what is lawful."***